1 MONTH OF
FREE
READING

at
www.ForgottenBooks.com

By purchasing this book you are eligible for one month membership to ForgottenBooks.com, giving you unlimited access to our entire collection of over 1,000,000 titles via our web site and mobile apps.

To claim your free month visit:
www.forgottenbooks.com/free1046362

ISBN 978-0-331-82055-3
PIBN 11046362

State of Rhode Island and Providence Plantations.

ANNUAL REPORT

OF THE

Rhode Island

GENERAL TREASURER,

Compliments of

Walter A. Read,

General Treasurer.

PROVIDENCE, R. I.
E. L. FREEMAN & SONS, STATE PRINTERS.
1906.

ANNUAL REPORT

OF THE

Rhode Is. Cand

GENERAL TREASURER,

MADE TO THE

GENERAL ASSEMBLY,

AT ITS

JANUARY SESSION, A. D. 1906.

PROVIDENCE, R. I.
E. L. FREEMAN & SONS, STATE PRINTERS.
1906.

GENERAL TREASURERS.

BEFORE THE PARLIAMENTARY PATENT.

PORTSMOUTH AND NEWPORT.

Treasurers.

Robert Jeoffreys, }
William Balston, } ....March 12, 1640, to March 16, 1641.

Robert Jeoffreys........................March 16, 1641, to March 16, 1642.

NEWPORT.

Robert Jeoffreys.......................March 16, 1641, to March 13, 1644.

Jeremy Clarke.........................March 13, 1644, to May 19, 1647.

PORTSMOUTH.

Thomas Spicer.........................March 16, 1642, to ——————

UNDER THE PARLIAMENTARY PATENT.

General Treasurers.

Jeremy Clarke, Newport....................May 19, 1647, to May 22, 1649.

John Clarke, Newport...,..................May 22, 1649, to the separation.

PROVIDENCE AND WARWICK.

Randall Holden, Warwick.........................May, 1652, to May, 1654.

PORTSMOUTH AND NEWPORT.

John Coggeshall, Newport....................May 17, 1653, to May 16, 1654.

UNION RE—ESTABLISHED.

John Coggeshall, Newport......................May 1654, to Sept. 12, 1654.

Richard Burden, Portsmouth................Sept. 12, 1654, to May 22, 1655.

John Sanford, Portsmouth...................May 22, 1655, to May 21, 1661.
Caleb Carr, Newport.........................May 21, 1661, to May 22, 1662.
John Sanford, Portsmouth...................May 22, 1662, to Nov. 25, 1663.

UNDER THE ROYAL CHARTER OF CHARLES II.

John Sanford, Portsmouth..................Nov. 26, 1663, to May 4, 1664.
John Coggeshall, Newport....................................1664 to 1672.
Peter Easton, Newport.......................................1672 to 1677.
Thomas Ward, Newport..1677 to 1678.
Peleg Sanford, Newport......................................1678 to 1681.
Weston Clarke, Newport......................................1681 to 1685.
*John Woodman, Newport......................................1685 to 1686.
John Holmes, Newport.......................February, 1690, to May, 1703.
William Hiscock, Newport....................................1703 to 1705.
Nathaniel Sheffield, Newport................................1705 to 1708.
John Holmes, Newport..1708 to 1709.
Edward Thurston, Newport....................................1709 to 1714.
Joseph Borden, Portsmouth...................................1714 to 1730.
Abraham Borden, Newport.....................................1730 to 1733.
Gideon Wanton, Newport......................................1733 to 1743.
John Gardner, Newport.......................................1743 to 1748.
Thomas Richardson, Newport..................................1748 to 1761.
Joseph Clarke, Newport............................1761 to 1792.   Died.
Henry Sherburne, Newport.................October, 1792, to May, 1808.
Constant Taber, Newport.....................................1808 to 1811.
William Ennis, Newport......................................1811 to 1817.
Thomas G. Pitman, Newport...................................1817 to 1832.
John Sterne, Newport..1832 to 1838.
William S. Nichols, Newport.................................1838 to 1839.
John Sterne, Newport..1839 to 1840.
Stephen Cahoone, Newport....................................1840 to 1843.

UNDER THE CONSTITUTION.

Stephen Cahoone, Newport....................................1843 to 1851.
Edwin Wilbur, Newport.......................................1851 to 1854.
Samuel B. Vernon, Newport...................................1854 to 1855.
Samuel A. Parker, Newport...................................1855 to 1866.

---

*At this date the charter was suspended by Sir Edmund Andros.

George W. Tew, Newport...........................May, 1866, to March, 1868.

Samuel A. Parker, Newport..............March, 1868, to Feb. 4, 1872.   Died.

Samuel Clark, Lincoln...............................Feb. 15, 1872, to 1887.

John G. Perry, South Kingstown.............................1887 to 1888.

Samuel Clark, Lincoln..1888 to 1890.

John G. Perry, South Kingstown.............................1890 to 1891.

Samuel Clark, Lincoln.......................1891 to Dec. 27, 1897.   Died.

Clinton D. Sellew, Providence...................Dec. 28, 1897, to May 31, 1898.

Walter A. Read, Glocester.....................................1898 to

---

TREASURY DEPARTMENT.

General Treasurer.............................Walter A. Read, of Glocester.

Bookkeeper....................................Charles C. Clark, of Lincoln.

Clerk............................. ......Hattie M. Fletcher, of Pawtucket.

REPORT.

General Treasurer's Office,

Providence, R. I., January 1, 1906.

To the Honorable General Assembly of the State of Rhode Island and Providence Plantations:

I submit herewith a detailed statement of the receipts and expenditures of the treasury department for the fiscal year ending December 31, 1905, in accordance with the provisions of Chapter 33, Title VI, of the General Laws.

It is gratifying to note that under the operation of the revaluation bill, passed by the General Assembly at its last session, the income of the State the past year has equalled its expenditures, and that it will provide sufficient revenue to meet the current expenses of 1906 if care and discrimination is made in appropriations for special objects.

The floating debt of the State amounting to $245,000.00, due and payable in 1906, should be kept in mind, and while it may not be possible to liquidate the debt in full from the receipts of this coming year, it is possible, as well as prudent, to provide at least for its reduction.

A detailed statement of the condition of the State House Sinking Fund, the Touro Jewish Synagogue Fund, the Land Grant Fund of 1862, and other funds in custody of the State, will be found in the Appendix, with a list of the unexpended balances of appropriations made by previous General Assemblies, and the sources of State revenue and the amount derived from each.

GENERAL ACCOUNT.

Balance in treasury January 1, 1905............................	$53,828 24
Receipts from January 1, 1905, to December 31, 1905...........	2,001,951 17
	$2,055,779 41

Payments from January 1, 1905, to December 31, 1905, on Regular Appropriations.............	$1,402,727 33	
Payments on Special Appropriations.............	450,667 51	
Payment to Sinking Fund......................	41,000 00	
Note cancelled at R. I. H. Trust Company........	50,000 00	
Balance in treasury December 31, 1905...........	111,384 57	
		$2,055,779 41

DEPOSITS.

Cash, Rhode Island Hospital Trust Company, interest 2 per cent. daily balances..	$85,968 65
Cash, Industrial Trust Company, interest 2 per cent. daily balances	25,290 61
Cash in hand..	125 31
	$111,384 57

RECEIPTS.

From January 1, 1905, to December 30, 1905, inclusive.

Tax Assignments..	$196,479 35
State Tax...	602,110 75
Institutions for Savings....................................	435,299 49
State Insurance Companies.................................	92,037 74
Foreign Insurance Agents..................................	127,004 63
Salary and Expenses of the Railroad Commissioner.............	4,000 00
Town Councils..	128,995 76
State Institutions in Cranston..............................	54,352 41
State Home and School....................................	600 45
School Fund Dividend.....................................	9,131 37
Charters...	38,217 50
Civil Commissions...	2,938 00
General Laws, Schedules, and Rhode Island Reports.	1,515 70
Peddlers' Licenses...	1,905 00
Auctioneers...	1,628 79
Commissioners of Shell Fisheries............................	47,087 26
Commercial Fertilizers.....................................	2,436 00
Interest on Deposits of the Revenue.........................	3,157 76
National Home for Disabled Volunteer Soldiers.................	13,374 84
Supreme Court..	13,175 56
District Court, First Judicial District.......................	3,277 85

District Court, Second Judicial District........................ 481 95
District Court, Third Judicial District......................... 503 70
District Court, Fourth Judicial District....................... 989 00
District Court, Fifth Judicial District......................... 1,267 35
District Court, Sixth Judicial District........................ 14,323 00
District Court, Seventh Judicial District...................... 950 25
District Court, Eighth Judicial District....................... 1,026 05
District Court, Ninth Judicial District........................ 210 15
District Court, Tenth Judicial District........................ 2,052 65
District Court, Eleventh Judicial District..................... 1,755 15
District Court, Twelfth Judicial District...................... 956 45
Jailers.. 6,277 57
Tax on Street Railway Companies............................... 60,478 12
Tax on Telephone Companies.................................... 7,600 31
Tax on Telegraph Companies.................................... 823 03
Tax on Express Companies...................................... 531 14
Construction and Improvement of State Highways................ 7,206 21
Tuition, Rhode Island Normal School........................... 5,692 91
Rent of old Normal School Building............................ 680 00
Proceeds from sales at Camp Ground, "R. I. M.".............. 260 00
Military and Naval Expenses, War with Spain................... 6,907 95
Notes... 95,000 00
Firemen's Relief Fund... 1,413 53
State Sanatorium for Consumptives............................. 500 02
Automobile and Motor Cycle Licenses........................... 1,684 00
Miscellaneous... 3,654 47

$2,001,951 17

PAYMENTS.—GROSS AMOUNTS.

Salaries.. $171,853 63
Executive Secretary... 1,200 00
Clerk of the Attorney-General................................. 500 00
Clerk, Commissioners of Shell Fisheries....................... 1,319 89
Additional clerk hire, Secretary of State..................... 1,200 00
Clerical Assistance, Secretary of State....................... 1,133 33
Clerical Assistance, Clerk, First District Court.............. 300 00
Clerical Assistance, Clerk, Sixth District Court.............. 1,500 00
Clerical Assistance, Adjutant-General......................... 1,500 00
Clerical Assistance, Quartermaster-General.................... 1,000 00
Clerical Assistance, Assistant Adjutant-General............... 500 00
Clerical Assistance, Clerk, Appellate and Common Pleas Division,
    Supreme Court, Newport County............................. 162 90
Clerical Assistance Superior Court, Newport County............ 137 10
Additional Clerical Assistance, Insurance Commissioner........ 1,600 00
Additional Clerical Assistance, Clerk of Common Pleas Division,
    Supreme Court, Providence County.......................... 2,025 30

2

Additional Clerical Assistance, General Treasurer	856	00
Clerk Hire and Incidentals, Law Library	499	18
Services of Watchman at Camp Ground	600	00
Janitor, Newport County Jail	500	00
Watchman, Newport County Jail	600	00
Janitor, Washington County Court House	500	00
Janitor, Bristol County Court House	75	00
Secretary of State Returning Board	1,000	00
Clerical Assistance, State Returning Board	410	00
Secretary, Commissioners of Inland Fisheries	600	00
State Registrar	1,000	00
State Librarian	1,127	95
Clerk Hire and Incidentals, State Librarian	500	00
Rhode Island Historical Society	1,500	00
Newport Historical Society	500	00
R. I. Society for Prevention of Cruelty to Children	2,500	00
R. I. Society for Prevention of Cruelty to Animals	1,000	00
Prisoners' Aid Association	1,000	00
Providence Lying-in Hospital	2,500	00
Rhode Island Horticultural Society	1,000	00
Rhode Island Poultry Association	1,000	00
Washington County Agricultural Society	1,000	00
Newport County Agricultural Society	1,000	00
Newport Horticultural Society	750	00
Messengers, New State House	2,000	00
Pay and Mileage of the General Assembly	37,722	84
Clerks of the General Assembly	3,000	00
Clerks of Committees, General Assembly	8,900	00
Officers, General Assembly	940	00
Pages, General Assembly	1,710	00
Doorkeepers, General Assembly	3,166	00
Stationery and Stamps, General Assembly	371	01
Accounts allowed by General Assembly	4,524	88
Advertising and Publishing Public Laws	5,650	62
Traveling Expenses, Justices of the Supreme Court	864	61
Traveling Expenses, Attorney-General and Assistant	60	49
Traveling Expenses, Stenographic Clerks	645	56
Furniture, &c., State Sealer	78	00
Court Stenographers, Supreme and Superior Courts	2,559	77
Saint Vincent De Paul Infant Asylum	2,500	00
Purchase of Publications R. I. Soldiers' and Sailors' Historical Society	61	20
Supervision of Public Schools	10,750	00
Printing and Binding Vol. 6, R. I. Reports	1,339	50
Expenses of J. S. Committee, Ballot Reform	1,095	31
Jurors, Supreme Court	47,752	84
Officers, Supreme and Superior Courts	22,059	45
Witnesses of Supreme Court	10,814	30

Incidental Expenses, Supreme Court	6,725 22
Officers, District Courts	12,991 15
Witnesses, Districts Courts	6,759 50
Officers in Criminal Cases	8,690 35
Rhode Island Normal School	63,999 76
Rhode Island Normal School (mileage)	4,000 00
Rhode Island School of Design	5,951 75
Public Schools	120,000 00
Graded and High Schools	17,630 00
Evening Schools	4,853 40
School Apparatus	3,575 63
Teachers' Institutes	110 75
Lectures and Addresses	164 01
Teachers' Examinations	2,264 48
Investment of Permanent School Fund	4,516 98
State Home and School	21,590 56
Rhode Island Institute for the Deaf	19,963 98
State Institutions in Cranston	342,387 19
State Board of Health	5,998 81
State Board of Agriculture	19,046 66
State Board of Public Roads	4,999 31
Maintenance of Rhode Island College of Agriculture	15,000 00
Public Libraries	7,486 75
State Library	397 61
Law Library	2,297 29
Indigent Insane	10,000 00
Education of Blind and Imbecile	15,997 51
Providence County Court House	4,498 71
Old State House, Providence	479 50
Woonsocket Court House	496 47
Public Buildings, Newport County	1,298 57
Public Buildings, Washington County	496 56
Public Buildings, Kent County	429 49
Public Buildings, Bristol County	313 02
Care of Old State House, Providence	1,500 00
Care of New State House, Providence	38,921 74
Care of State House, Newport	533 33
Care of Providence County Court House	6,632 73
Care of Woonsocket Court House	1,200 00
Care of District Court Rooms	404 00
Care of Military Burial Ground, Dutch Island	12 50
Transfer of Battle Flags	555 62
Repairs and Improvements, State Buildings, Charlestown	300 00
Care of Soldiers' and Sailors' Monument, Providence	50 00
Care of Perry Monument, Newport	30 00
Care of Stephen Hopkins Monument	25 00
State Printing	39,999 62
State Binding	8,994 00

Militia and Military Affairs.	37,499 84
Rifle Practice, State Militia.	4,999 83
Armory Rents, R. I. Militia.	7,141 03
Heating and Lighting Armories.	3,300 00
Storage and Care of Equipments, R. I. Militia.	700 00
Markers for Soldiers' and Sailors' Graves.	206 20
Colonial and Revolutionary War Records.	431 35
Miscellaneous Expenses.	12,000 00
Medical Examiners and Coroners.	4,999 74
Control and Prevention of Tuberculosis.	1,496 16
Cause and Prevention of Diphtheria.	1,758 74
Jails and Jailers.	1,470 02
Fuel and Gas.	10,621 77
Rents.	1,658 25
Fines in Certain Cases.	2,028 00
Inland Fisheries.	7,682 23
Orders of the Governor, "Civil Account".	2,534 67
Orders of the Governor "Criminal Account".	524 29
Soldiers' Home Fund.	37,482 51
Soldiers' Relief Fund.	9,843 00
Commissioners of Sinking Fund.	41,000 00
Interest on Bonds, State House Construction Loan.	87,000 00
Interest on Temporary Loans.	15,508 50
Interest on Land Grant Fund, 1862.	534 22
Commercial Fertilizers.	2,200 61
Commercial Feeding Stuffs.	1,194 59
Expenses Enforcing Laws Relative to Shell Fisheries.	1,180 00
Expenses of Factory Inspectors.	556 34
Expenses of Commissioners of Birds.	264 36
Expenses of Commissioner, Industrial Statistics.	2,999 26
State Sanatorium.	48,126 78
Expenses, State Record Commissioner.	594 39
Expenses, State Board of Soldiers' Relief.	1,093 22
Expenses, Commissioner of Dams, &c.	160 00
Expenses, Commissioners on Uniformity of Legislation.	200 00
Expenses, Attorney-General's Department.	863 76
Expenses, Railroad Commissioner.	633 04
Expenses, State Returning Board.	1,013 44
Construction and Furnishing State Hospital for the Insane.	4,271 45
Providence Armory.	1,000 00
Bounty for Wild Foxes.	194 00
Bounty for Wild Crows, Hawks, &c.	415 25
State Sanatorium for Consumptives.	25,500 02
Furnishing Old State House for Sixth District Court.	160 00
Proceeds of Camp Ground, R. I. Militia.	383 19
State Representation at Expositions and Celebrations.	2,494 96
Expenses of Opening Breachway at Block Island.	952 00
Expenses of Opening Breachway at South Kingstown.	123 12

Reclaiming Burial Place, Governor Benedict Arnold............ 15 00
Industrial Education at Sockanosset School.................... 489 83
Note, R. I. H. Trust Company, cancelled..................... 50,000 00
Grading and Improving Land at Indian Burial Ground Hill...... 39 15
Preservation of Land Titles, Kent and Washington Counties..... 11 20
Protection of Devil's Breach at Charlestown Pond.............. 336 57
Law Library, Supreme Court........................ 1,702 18
Expenses of Rhode Island Stone Bridge Commission............ 53,969 96
Newspaper Records of Early Deaths in Rhode Island........... 2,000 00
Repairing State Armory, East Greenwich...................... 128 32
Repairing Heating Apparatus, Bristol Armory................. 930 00
Supreme Court Commission................................ 2,344 77
Temporary Quarters, Supreme Court........................ 72,162 34
Louisiana Purchase Exposition............................. 2,703 92
Instruction of Adult Blind................................ 1,912 49
Repairing and Furnishing Providence County Court House....... 33 38
Construction of Inner Harbor Block Island 128 81
Agricultural Demonstrations.............................. 3,680 06
Repairs and Improvements, Rhode Island College of Agriculture.. 2,155 01
State Shipping Interests in Providence Harbor................. 684 37
Construction and Improvement of State Roads................. 100,339 54
Expenses of Metropolitan Park Commission.................... 957 27
Repairing State Arsenal, Providence......................... 1,225 30
Repairing Newport County Jail............................. 194 00
Expenses of State Sealer................................. 27 86
Repairs and Alterations, State Rifle Range................... 1,100 00
Compensation of Supreme Court Commission.................... 17,500 00
Expenses of Shell Fish Commissioners Investigating Pollution of
    Providence River...................................... 1,200 94
U. S. Volunteer Life Saving Corps.......................... 170 34
Purchase of Library of the late Geo. F. Keene, M. D........... 1,200 00
Deficiency Account, Rhode Island College of Agriculture......... 5,000 00
Repairing Newport County Court House...................... 1,032 56
State Census, 1905....................................... 18,939 37

$1,944,394 84

Tax Assignments, due June 15, 1905.

	Tax.	Discount.	Net Amount.
Central Falls.............	$7,827 90	$18 26	$7,809 64
Pawtucket.............	33,895 24	79 09	33,816 15
Woonsocket.............	15,366 02	35 85	15,330 17
Warwick.............	16,924 28	39 49	16,884 79
East Providence.............	8,500 11	11 57	8,488 54
Cumberland.............	7,741 64	10 54	7,731 10
Cranston.............	12,429 84	16 92	12,412 92
Westerly.............	6,231 80	8 48	6,223 32
	$108,916 83	$220 20	$108,696 63

State Tax, due June 15, 1905.

Narragansett	$3,328 59
Exeter	490 64
South Kingstown	4,680 15
Little Compton	1,294 08
North Kingstown	3,900 03
Scituate	2,165 22
Jamestown	2,330 67
Richmond	1,097 06
Warren	4,134 02
Coventry	3,562 00
Middletown	2,742 59
Charlestown	754 07
Tiverton	2,730 36
Burrillville	3,517 70
Portsmouth	2,609 57
North Smithfield	1,773 15
Newport	38,732 04
Lincoln	4,245 59
Bristol	5,242 95
Smithfield	1,516 57
Johnston	2,266 40
Glocester	980 37
Foster	452 58
Providence	187,185 26
Barrington	2,452 42
East Greenwich	2,087 37
West Greenwich	320 48
North Providence	1,593 50
Hopkinton	1,602 50
New Shoreham	805 68
	$290,593 61

Tax Assignments, due December 15, 1905.

	Tax.	Discount.	Net Amount.
Newport	$38,732 04	$107 59	$38,624 45
Pawtucket	33,895 24	79 09	33,816 15
Woonsocket	15,366 02	23 90	15,342 12
	$87,993 30	$210 58	$87,782 72

State Tax, due December 15, 1905.

Johnston	$2,266 40
Bristol	5,242 95
North Providence	1,593 50

Richmond	1,097	05
Narragansett	3,328	59
Hopkinton	1,602	50
Little Compton	1,294	08
South Kingstown	4,680	15
Middletown	2,742	59
Exeter	490	64
West Greenwich	320	48
Warren	4,134	02
Coventry	3,562	00
Scituate	2,165	22
Jamestown	2,330	67
Cumberland	7,741	64
East Greenwich	2,087	37
North Smithfield	1,773	15
Charlestown	754	07
Foster	452	58
Central Falls	7,827	90
Portsmouth	2,609	57
Smithfield	1,516	57
Burrillville	3,517	70
Warwick	16,924	28
Providence	187,185	26
Cranston	12,429	84
East Providence	8,500	11
Barrington	2,452	42
North Kingstown	3,900	03
Glocester	980	37
Tiverton	2,730	36
Lincoln	4,245	59
Westerly	6,231	80
New Shoreham	805	68
	$311,517	**14**

Recapitulation.

	Tax.	Discount.	Net Amount.
Tax Assignment Orders, due June 15, 1905	$108,916 83	$220 20	$108,696 63
Tax Assignment Orders, due December 15, 1905	87,993 30	210 58	87,782 72
	$196,910 13	$430 78	$196,479 35
State Tax, due June 15, 1905	290,593 61	....	290,593 61
State Tax, due December 15, 1905	311,517 14	....	311,517 14
	$799,020 88	$430 78	$798,590 10

Institutions for Savings.

Ashaway Savings Bank, Ashaway	* $227 60
Centreville Savings Bank, Centreville	1,498 52
Citizens Savings Bank, Providence	34,063 59
Coddington Savings Bank, Newport	2,056 28
Island Savings Bank, Newport	4,258 75
Kingston Savings Bank, Kingston	1,452 88
Mechanics Savings Bank, Providence	7,142 97
Mechanics Savings Bank, Woonsocket	4,300 99
Niantic Savings Bank, Westerly	7,504 50
Pawtucket Institution for Savings, Pawtucket	20,208 50
Peoples Savings Bank, Providence	23,755 53
Peoples Savings Bank, Woonsocket	7,316 90
Producers Savings Bank, Woonsocket	6,524 49
Providence County Savings Bank, Pawtucket	3,680 43
Providence Institution for Savings, Providence	75,304 14
Savings Bank of Newport, Newport	29,389 60
Smithfield Savings Bank, Greenville	2,277 74
Wakefield Institution for Savings, Wakefield	3,001 20
Warren Institution for Savings, Warren	5,164 42
Westerly Savings Bank, Westerly	422 76
Wickford Savings Bank, Wickford	1,394 16
Woonsocket Institution for Savings, Woonsocket	26,493 52
Central Trust Company, Providence	176 26
Industrial Trust Company, Providence	69,657 99
Manufacturers Trust Company, Providence	14,671 09
New England Trust Company, Providence	712 01
Pawtucket Trust Company, Pawtucket	4 02
Phenix Trust Company, Phenix	458 44
R. I. Hospital Trust Company, Providence	41,543 10
Slater Trust Company, Pawtucket	11,373 90
Union Trust Company, Providence	20,672 80
Wakefield Trust Company, Wakefield	51 29
Washington Trust Company, Westerly	8,539 12
	$435,299 49

State Insurance Companies.

American Mutual Fire Insurance Company	$3,736 88
Aquidneck Mutual Fire Insurance Company	90 34
Blackstone Mutual Fire Insurance Company	8,615 66
Enterprise Mutual Fire Insurance Company	3,741 08
Firemens Mutual Fire Insurance Company	11,909 30
Franklin Mutual Fire Insurance Company	147 36
Hope Mutual Fire Insurance Company	5,532 88
Manufacturers Mutual Fire Insurance Company	6,932 56
Mechanics Mutual Fire Insurance Company	4,902 30

Merchants Mutual Fire Insurance Company	4,433	48
Mercantile Mutual Fire Insurance Company	3,069	38
Metal Workers Mutual Fire Insurance Company	758	66
Narragansett Mutual Fire Insurance Company	1,988	88
Patrons Fire Relief Association	23	66
Pawtucket Mutual Fire Insurance Company	1,351	60
Providence Mutual Fire Insurance Company	979	34
Rhode Island Mutual Fire Insurance Company	9,146	40
State Mutual Fire Insurance Company	13,858	54
Textile Manufacturers Mutual Fire Insurance Company	880	52
Tiverton and Little Compton Mutual Fire Insurance Company	17	64
Union Mutual Fire Insurance Company	581	14
What Cheer Mutual Fire Insurance Company	6,124	40
Hope Live Stock Mutual Fire Insurance Company	176	58
Equitable Fire and Marine Insurance Company	631	20
Providence Washington Insurance Company	2,090	78
Providence Life Insurance Company	103	46
Health and Accident Security Company	65	22
Underwriters at New England Lloyds	148	50
	$92,037	74

Foreign Insurance Agents.

Herbert B. Horton		28
Fagan & Moore	5	12
William R. Randall	34	65
P. Skinner, Jr.	120	96
James G. Topham	62	90
Adolphus Brownell		05
Charlotte E. Rice	2	17
C. Frank Parkhurst	38	17
Anna L. Palmer	2	10
Edward M. Burke	2	61
W. W. Logee	145	39
William H. Herrick	115	30
Walter L. Kelley	18	98
A. Lincoln Hambly	36	40
Moses E. Shippee	174	58
Franklin Porter	1	28
William M. P. Bowen	55	35
New York Life Insurance Company	6,051	50
William F. Caswell	3	64
William H. Draper	12	56
William H. Draper	1	02
George N. Girard	167	53
C. A. Morgan	706	37
Joseph T. Day	14	27
Arnold & Tillinghast	262	23

A. P. White.. 179 97
Byron H. Nixon... 25
A. O'D. Taylor... 21 24
Laura C. Dennis.. 26
Herbert R. Perkins... 64 26
C. H. Straight... 3 50
Henry W. Cooke Company.. 247 38
Olin Hill.. 11 39
John D. Turner... 9 16
Mutual Reserve Life Insurance Company......................... 309 58
Fidelity Mutual Life Insurance Company........................ 135 02
Marcoux Brothers.. 68
New England Mutual Life Insurance Company..................... 1,973 04
Frank W. Coy... 89 09
Charles E. Boon & Co... 80 80
J. L. Sanders.. 15 14
George H. Bunce.. 276 14
Thomas A. Gardner.. 51 09
Alfred U. Eddy... 168 04
Charles H. Philbrick... 169 26
Frederick H. Paine... 174 50
Zenas W. Bliss... 23 50
Charles H. Philbrick... 18 68
Stephen C. Harris.. 14 49
Home Life Insurance Company.................................... 222 44
G. A. Spink.. 3 51
John C. Budlong, Jr.. 20 15
George H. Peck... 18 98
Theodore P. Bogert... 827 56
John H. Arnold... 26 86
George T. Baker.. 1 00
B. M. MacDougall... 6 46
Howard W. Farnum... 3 76
Walter H. Crowninshield.. 11 22
Union Mutual Life Insurance Company............................ 401 83
William H. Draper.. 93
Robert L. Gaskill.. 49 98
H. M. Clarke... 9 68
Edward S. Babbitt.. 393 76
The Standard Life & Accident Insurance Company................. 90 34
Hjalmer Norberg.. 14 80
James W. Cook.. 214 56
James W. Cook.. 9 71
John Hancock Mutual Life Insurance Company..................... 12,110 28
Stephen H. Brown... 24 10
Henry W. Cooke Company... 190 14
Kirby R. Brockenbrough... 697 46
John E. Babcock.. 32 09

Charles A. Pettingill..	45	53
J. J. Luther...	237	07
James W. Stainton...	39	82
Joseph P. Canning...	248	38
The Washington Life Insurance Company....................	295	62
Aylesworth & Hood...		50
G. L. & H. J. Gross..	814	40
Isaac A. Shippee..	7	41
Thomas O'Brien..	3	39
John Eddy & Son...	312	65
Elmer C. Mason..	143.	08
DeBlois & Eldredge..	720	65
Eugene A. Tingley...	32	79
Equitable Life Assurance Society of the United States..........	6,237	58
United States Casualty Company............................	40	16
Snow & Barker...	1,026	45
Albert Babcock..	262	23
C. E. Roberts...	231	42
Isaac L. Goff...	414	44
Barney & Carpenter..	8	31
Henry B. Simmons..	116	26
Elmer C. Mason..	7	59
The United States Life Insurance Company..................	26	15
James J. Rooney...	4	03
William E. Williams.......................................	855	66
The Mutual Benefit Life Insurance Company.................	1,429	96
Fred E. Horton..	4	99
Richard F. Aust...		46
Patrick F. Kinion...	7	13
Chase & Entwistle...	65	14
Matthew J. Gallagher......................................	87	55
The Fidelity & Casualty Company of New York...............	1,336	17
Henry Bull, Jr..	1,457	67
Thomas J. Rowen...		29
Penn Mutual Life Insurance Company........................	729	76
Northwestern Mutual Life Insurance Company................	2,916	24
Ætna Life Insurance Company...............................	619	58
Frank B. Knowles..	3	43
The Prudential Insurance Company of America...............	4,230	84
Frederick H. Jackson......................................	7,096	86
J. A. Keach...	344	78
Joseph T. A. Eddy...	586	91
Charles A. Tompkins.......................................	48	96
Frank X. Roberts & Son....................................	22	23
D. C. Sweet & Company.....................................	634	11
James H. Sweet..	1,017	17
Howard B. Perry...	27	73
Elmer W. Shippee..	12	68

Roscoe L. Colman...	2,454 74
Roscoe L. Colman...	142 21
William C. Mowry..	130 34
John Shuttleworth..	66 44
William P. Clancy..	20 12
A. L. Chester..	74 60
Jeremiah Purtill..	1 33
W. A. Lester...	1,312 23
Stephen J. Casey...	38 81
John B. McGuinness..	90 34
Edward H. Farnum...	79 05
R. P. Smith & Son...	870 54
A. N. Morin & Son...	101 91
Spencer & Boss..	162 73
Spencer & Boss..	1,269 77
A. W. Godding...	4 04
The Mass. Mutual Life Insurance Company....................	4,535 47
Richard A. Hurley..	16 70
C. F. Newcomb...	577 18
Walter E. Munroe..	463 32
Frederick P. Church..	2 94
Ralph C. Watrous & Company................................	56 58
Ralph C. Watrous & Company................................	15 19
Henry W. Cooke & Company.................................	11 94
H. G. Wilks...	16 40
Clarence A. Hammett.......................................	195 39
The Colonial Assurance Company............................	14 10
Thomas J. O'Neill..	31 59
Isaac Shove Company.......................................	484 33
Irvine O. Chester..	79 35
Holden & Greene...	181 87
William S. Todd..	6 83
William C. Chambers.......................................	73 83
F. R. Dooley, for Dennis & Sawyer..........................	8 55
Charles C. Cook...	3 84
John L. Borden..	3 19
Charles L. Hazard..	39 59
Frank G. Combes...	110 21
S. A. Nightingale & Company................................	12 37
Frank R. Dooley...	4 62
C. W. Davis...	14 39
Adelbert Goff..	7 76
Charles M. Moore..	42
Metropolitan Life Insurance Company........................	18,724 33
Employers Liability Assurance Corporation, "Ltd."..........	545 46
New York Security & Trust Company.........................	376 59
The Security Trust & Life Insurance Company of Philadelphia....	177 88
Charles A. Leach...	2 20

John F. J. O'Connor	28	73
Joseph Perkins, Jr.	47	71
Robert Young	8	91
Thomas A. Pingree	22	80
A. H. Sunderland	2	02
A. C. Purdy	51	72
James J. Williams		45
Hartford Life Insurance Company	219	03
C. H. Wrightington	45	95
C. S. Packer	9	91
William E. Brightman	463	84
Edward McCabe & Son	21	32
Walter D. Harris	27	21
American Credit Indemnity Company	261	23
George H. Olney	8	78
William A. Baggott	39	67
Frankfort Marine, Accident & Plate Glass Insurance Company	133	00
Gamwell & Ingraham	91	39
Walter E. Grey	192	37
R. W. Thompson	877	27
Walter E. Grey	1	00
United States Health & Accident Insurance Company	4	57
The Life Association of America	9	96
United States Guarantee Company	1	36
J. E. Walsh	4	23
Charles J. Flynn	1	94
Reliance Life Insurance Company	4	41
Harold C. Spencer		44
Starkweather & Shepley	7,503	95
H. F. Richards & Brother	83	34
Arthur O'Leary	839	16
George I. Parker	2	55
The Provident Life & Trust Company of Philadelphia	762	62
H. E. Watjen & Company	115	76
George I. Parker	127	36
Leo. F. Nadeau	92	58
Charles E. Holmes	2	40
Gallivan & O'Donnell	1,195	33
Ætna Life Insurance Company	578	67
George I. Parker	274	58
Richard A. Butler	10	14
Nicholas J. Golden		15
William H. Hall	11	72
State Mutual Life Assurance Company	366	65
Manhattan Life Insurance Company	419	30
Niagara Fire Insurance Company	2	51
George N. Durfee	12	48
Columbian National Life Insurance Company	717	02

Connecticut General Life Insurance Company	29	14
Dutchess Insurance Company	4	61
Home Fire & Marine Insurance Company	31	79
Union Central Life Insurance Company	907	11
Commercial Union Fire Insurance Company of New York	30	32
Williamsburgh City Fire Insurance Company	2	26
Abraham Manchester	2	07
C. B. Bliven		96
North River Insurance Company	27	19
The Farmers Fire Insurance Company	5	39
Firemens Insurance Company of Newark	9	89
Sun Insurance Office of London	19	66
Traders & Mechanics Mutual Fire Insurance Company	9	04
Merchants & Farmers Mutual Fire Insurance Company	4	12
Dorchester Mutual Fire Insurance Company	7	50
State Fire Insurance Company, Ltd., of Liverpool	6	31
Great Eastern Casualty & Indemnity Company	29	42
Commercial Union Assurance Company, Ltd	31	84
Phœnix Assurance Company, Ltd	8	52
The Philadelphia Casualty Company	7	29
John O'Donnell	68	34
Beach & Sweet	2,095	40
Northern Insurance Company	8	61
London Guarantee & Accident Company	3	73
Standard Life & Accident Insurance Company	39	23
New Amsterdam Casualty Company	73	33
D. C. Sweet & Company	2	65
E. F. Mulligan	78	27
Myles M. Mulligan	82	53
Fidelity & Deposit Company of Maryland	142	42
The Home Insurance Company	24	54
Norwich Union Fire Insurance Society	11	26
Northern Assurance Company	3	61
Ætna Insurance Company	26	59
Hartford Fire Insurance Company	7	62
Hanover Fire Insurance Company	35	49
American Central Insurance Company	56	43
Teutonia Insurance Company	16	50
Germania Fire Insurance Company	7	61
Metropolitan Plate Glass & Casualty Insurance Company	15	88
New Hampshire Fire Insurance Company	10	95
The Empire State Surety Company	1	94
Fire Association of Philadelphia	1	70
Maryland Casualty Company	192	94
Loyal Protective Association	81	48
Rubber Manufacturers Mutual Insurance Company	9	85
Cotton & Woolen Manufacturers Mutual Fire Insurance Company	7	02
Industrial Mutual Insurance Company	4	35

The New York Plate Glass Insurance Company..................	1	09
The General Accident Assurance Corporation, Ltd..............	60	79
Insurance Company of North America........................	244	87
Camden Fire Insurance Association.........................	59	58
Glens Falls Fire Insurance Company........................	2	13
Travelers Life Insurance Company..........................	38	23
Travelers Accident Insurance Company......................	3	14
Atlas Assurance Company, Ltd.............................	3	42
Protective Disability Insurance Company....................	35	10
Charles C. Gray, Insurance Commissioner, "Insurance Fees"......	9,000	00
Charles C. Gray, Insurance Commissioner, "Insurance Fees"......	4,192	80
	$129,504	63
Amount paid for Firemen's Relief Fund under the provisions of Chapter 1161, Public Laws...............................	2,500	00
	$127,004	63

Town Councils.

Town Treasurer, North Providence, for liquor licenses...........	$625	00
Town Treasurer, North Providence, for pool tables, etc...........	50	00
Town Treasurer, Cumberland, for liquor licenses.................	2,725	50
City Treasurer, Newport, for liquor licenses....................	7,886	16
City Treasurer, Newport, for billiard and pool tables, etc.........	571	50
City Treasurer, Providence, for liquor licenses.................	60,150	00
City Treasurer, Providence, for shows, billiards, etc.............	2,890	50
City Treasurer, Pawtucket, for liquor licenses.................	11,831	62
Town Treasurer, Foster, for liquor licenses....................	100	00
Town Treasurer, Warren, for liquor licenses...................	1,420	75
Town Treasurer, Cranston, for liquor licenses..................	1,125	00
Town Treasurer, Coventry, for liquor licenses..................	681	05
Town Treasurer, North Kingstown, for billiards, shows, etc.......	19	50
Town Treasurer, New Shoreham, for pool tables, bowling, etc.....	40	00
Town Treasurer, Westerly, for billiards, pool tables, etc..........	27	00
Town Treasurer, Johnston, for pool tables, etc..................	5	00
Town Treasurer, Warwick, for liquor licenses..................	5,724	37
Town Treasurer, Warwick, for pool tables and shows............	9	15
Town Treasurer, Scituate, for liquor licenses..................	175	00
Town Treasurer, Scituate, for exhibitions and socials............	42	50
Town Treasurer, South Kingstown, for pool tables, bowling, etc...	54	50
Town Treasurer, Lincoln, for pool tables, shows, etc.............	17	00
Town Treasurer, North Kingstown, for pool tables, shows, etc.....	27	00
City Treasurer, Pawtucket, for billiards, pool, bowling, etc........	696	50
Town Treasurer, Coventry, for liquor licenses..................	762	39
Town Treasurer, Coventry, for socials, etc.....................	2	00
City Treasurer, Woonsocket, for liquor licenses.................	327	29
City Treasurer, Woonsocket, for pool, bowling, shows, etc........	211	00

Town Treasurer, Bristol, for liquor licenses.....................	129	62
Town Treasurer, Cumberland, for socials, etc....................	9	50
Town Treasurer, Burrillville, for pool tables, socials, etc..........	74	25
Town Treasurer, Glocester, for liquor licenses....................	39	18
Town Treasurer, Glocester, for socials, etc......................	8	00
Town Treasurer, East Providence, for liquor licenses.............	1,350	00
Town Treasurer, East Providence, for pool tables, etc............	369	00
Town Treasurer, Cranston, for liquor licenses...................	37	50
Town Treasurer, Cranston, for pool tables, bowling, etc..........	77	50
City Treasurer, Central Falls, for liquor licenses.................	674	77
City Treasurer, Central Falls, for pool tables and socials.........	46	50
Town Treasurer, Johnston, for liquor licenses...................	50	26
Town Treasurer, Narragansett, for liquor licenses................	575	00
Town Treasurer, Johnston, for socials and exhibitions............	22	50
Town Treasurer, Warren, for pool and billiard tables, shows, etc..	60	00
Town Treasurer, Westerly, for pool tables, shows, etc............	54	50
Town Treasurer, Warwick, for liquor licenses....................	261	79
Town Treasurer, Cumberland, for liquor licenses.................	115	00
City Treasurer, Providence, for liquor licenses..................	1,300	00
City Treasurer, Providence, for pool and billiard tables, etc.......	3,964	00
Town Treasurer, North Smithfield, for liquor licenses............	62	50
City Treasurer, Pawtucket, for liquor licenses..................	144	96
Town Treasurer, North Providence, for liquor licenses............	562	50
Town Treasurer, North Providence, for socials, etc...............	30	00
Town Treasurer, Tiverton, for pool tables, etc...................	15	00
City Treasurer, Newport, for liquor licenses....................	390	62
City Treasurer, Newport, for shows, billiards, etc...............	375	50
Town Treasurer, Charlestown, for pool tables, bowling, etc........	7	50
Town Treasurer, Cumberland, for socials, etc....................	5	00
Town Treasurer, Narragansett, for liquor licenses................	225	83
Town Treasurer, Narragansett, for pool tables, etc...............	21	00
Town Treasurer, Scituate, for liquor licenses....................	200	00
Town Treasurer, Scituate, for socials, etc......................	8	50
City Treasurer, Pawtucket, for pool and billiard tables, etc.......	280	00
City Treasurer, Woonsocket, for pool tables, shows, etc..........	101	75
Town Treasurer, Warwick, for liquor licenses...................	5,611	98
Town Treasurer, Warwick, for pool tables, bowling, etc..........	25	00
Town Treasurer, East Providence, for shows, bowling, etc........	182	00
City Treasurer, Central Falls, for liquor licenses................	5,540	63
City Treasurer, Central Falls, for pool tables and shows.........	36	00
Town Treasurer, East Greenwich, for liquor licenses.............	843	75
Town Treasurer, Hopkinton, for shows, etc.....................	2	00
Town Treasurer, Bristol, for liquor licenses....................	1,681	25
Town Treasurer, Bristol, for pool and billiards, shows, etc........	57	50
Town Treasurer, Burrillville, for liquor licenses.................	1,887	50
Town Treasurer, Burrillville, for pool tables, shows, etc..........	70	67
Town Treasurer, Cranston, for liquor licenses...................	1,412	50
Town Treasurer, Glocester, for liquor licenses..................	150	00

Town Treasurer, Glocester, for pool tables, bowling, etc..........	18	50
Town Treasurer, Coventry, for liquor licenses...................	504	17
Town Treasurer, Coventry, for pool tables, socials, etc...........	6	00
Town Treasurer, Johnston, for liquor licenses..................	1,075	00
Town Treasurer, Johnston, for socials, bowling alleys, etc........	44	50
	$128,995	76

Charters.

The Williams & Anderson Company........................	$100	00
Principe di Piemonte..	5	00
Lewis J. Pierce Building Company...........................	100	00
Critic Club..	5	00
Davis Automobile Company, "Incorporated"..................	100	00
Olympia Social and Literary Club...........................	5	00
Oscar E. Place & Sons Company......	100	00
The Obstetrical Supply Company...........................	100	00
The Suburban Club...	5	00
Providence Building Trades Employers' Association.............	5	00
Spencer Yarn Company......................................	100	00
Guglielma Marconi Independent Political Club.................	5	00
The Edward E. Dammers Company..........................	100	00
Roger Williams Benevolent Association of Rhode Island.........	5	00
The Rhode Island Association of Graduate Nurses..............	5	00
The National Band of Natick, R. I...........................	5	00
E. K. Watson Company.....................................	125	00
The Vanholden Manufacturing Company......................	100	00
United Hebrew Citizens Association of Rhode Island............	5	00
Andrews & Spelman Company................................	100	00
United Creameries & Live Stock Company....................	100	00
Newport Realty Company...................................	100	00
Providence, Newport & Block Island Transportation Company.....	100	00
Providence Boys Club......................................	5	00
Societa Ufficiali di Marina Duca degli Abruzzi.................	5	00
Art Metal Milling Machine Company.........................	100	00
Royal Weaving Company, "Increase"........................	1,000	00
Merchants Co-operative Stamp Company......................	100	00
The Grand Lodge of the Degree of Honor, A. O. U. W., of Massachusetts...	5	00
Moosup Valley Church......................................	5	00
New England Lumber Company..............................	100	00
Valley Falls Athletic Club..................................	5	00
Charlestown Club..	5	00
Circle Montcalm...	5	00
Miantonomi Club...	5	00
Narragansett Brewing Company, "Increase"...................	250	00
The South Woodlawn Improvement Society...................	5	00
First Ward Colored Republican Club.........................	5	00

Flint Motor Car Company	100	00
Eastern Nail Company	100	00
Nicholson File Company, "Increase"	5,000	00
Narragansett Breeders Association	300	00
Industrial Trust Company, "Increase"	3,000	00
Lindsley & Allen Electric Company	100	00
The Hatchet Club	5	00
St. Vincent de Paul Home, Woonsocket, Rhode Island	100	00
Beacon Hill Land Company	100	00
Ninigret Country Club	5	00
Woonsocket Hebrew Mutual Aid Association	5	00
Providence Telephone Company, "Increase"	2,000	00
Royal Entertainers Club	5	00
Prudential Realty Company	100	00
Samsy Manufacturing Company	100	00
Consumers Rubber Company	100	00
Rhode Island Transcendent Light Company	100	00
Leonidas Social Club	5	00
Newport Social Club	5	00
Narragansett Finishing Company	100	00
The Newport Gas Light Company, "Increase"	200	00
Cameron Motor Boat Company	100	00
The Riverdale Republican Club	5	00
Falcon Worsted Company	100	00
H. B. Rust Company	100	00
John J. Clark & Company	100	00
Cutler Comb Company	100	00
Ninth Ward Protective Club	5	00
The City Hall Beneficial Association of Providence, Rhode Island	5	00
Pawtuxet Canoe Club	5	00
Union Hardware & Electric Supply Company, "Increase"	100	00
Peckham Brothers Company	100	00
Kingston Trust Company	100	00
The Dreadnaught Hook, Ladder and Hose Company	5	00
Fessenden & Company, "Incorporated"	100	00
Hale Clip & Fastener Company	100	00
Emanuel Parish Association	5	00
Colonial Trust Company	500	00
Starkweather & Shepley, "Incorporated"	100	00
The Congregation Ohawe Sholam of Pawtucket, Rhode Island	5	00
Massie Wireless Telegraph Company	100	00
The Herald Company	100	00
The Mathewson Company	100	00
The Club Franco-Republicain de Woodlawn, Pawtucket, R. I	5	00
The Flossette Mills Company	150	00
Fulton Land Company	100	00
Otis Brothers Company	100	00
The Union Club of Newport	5	00

The Thornton Club...	5	00
Equitable Trust Company.....................................	500	00
Sherry Casino Company.......................................	300	00
Eureka Social Club, East Providence..........................	5	00
Newport Co-operative Association for Saving and Building, "Increase"..	200	00
George L. Paine Company.....................................	100	00
The Consolidated Fish Company...............................	100	00
Branch Alliance of the First Congregational Church of Providence, Rhode Island...	5	00
William H. Herrick Company..................................	100	00
Warwick Neck Land Company.................................	100	00
The New York Hardware Company.............................	100	00
Narragansett Electric Lighting Company, "Increase"............	2,000	00
Rhode Island Insurance Company..............................	500	00
Wolcott Manufacturing Company..............................	100	00
East Side Hospital and Training School for Nurses..............	5	00
T. F. Irons Company...	100	00
Hope Webbing Company, "Increase"...........................	500	00
Providence Gas Company, "Increase"..........................	1,750	00
Equitable Loan and Investment Company.......................	100	00
Tiverton Gas Company..	100	00
Reliance Lubricator and Supply Company......................	100	00
Vasa Music Hall Association..................................	5	00
The State Printing and Publishing Company...................	100	00
Worcester & Providence Street Railway Company...............	1,000	00
Associated Merchants Stamp Company.........................	100	00
Fraternal Order of Eagles, Pawtucket Aerie, No. 796...........	5	00
The Supreme Lodge of the Provident Fraternity................	5	00
Hunter Club...	5	00
James S. Linton Company, "Ltd".............................	100	00
Waiters League Club...	5	00
What Cheer Grocery...	100	00
Rhode Island Loan and Investment Company...................	100	00
The Social Club...	5	00
Point Judith Railroad Company...............................	100	00
Berkeley Excelsior Social Club................................	5	00
The Columbia Social and Political Club.......................	5	00
Empire Machine Company.....................................	100	00
Societa Italiano Di Mutuo Umberto II Di Savoia Eriditario Di Italia	5	00
United Lace & Braid Manufacturing Company.................	100	00
Doe & Little Company..	100	00
Providence Steel & Iron Company.............................	100	00
Macedonia Baptist Church....................................	5	00
The Crescent Club...	5	00
The Rhode Island Company, "Increase".......................	665	00
Oakdale Manufacturing Company..............................	300	00
The Wonder Churn Company..................................	100	00

H. F. Horton & Sons Company	100 00
Newport Foundry & Machine Corporation	100 00
New England Linen Company	150 00
Standard Investment Company	100 00
The Lockwood Club	5 00
J. A. Foster Company Employees' Association	5 00
The C. W. Nass Company	100 00
Lincoln Republican Association	5 00
The Atlas Social Club	5 00
Saint Andrews Society of Newport, Rhode Island	5 00
Atlantic Mills of Rhode Island	1,000 00
Whittle Dye Works, "Increase"	200 00
Ellis Thayer Company	100 00
The Providence Wrecking Company	100 00
The Heirs of Thomas Burgess, "Incorporated"	212 50
Crooker Mantel & Tile Company	100 00
Household Furniture Company	100 00
Mount Hope Company	100 00
Washington Manufacturing Company	100 00
Wood River Country Club	5 00
Woonsocket Dyeing & Bleaching Company	100 00
Times Publishing Company, "Increase"	50 00
J. Fred Gibson Company	100 00
Lincoln Park Club	5 00
Bay View Club	5 00
Ring Paper Clip Company	100 00
The E. L. White Company	100 00
The Dexter Engineering Company	100 00
S. A. Harris Realty Company	100 00
The Armenian Reading Room	5 00
The Barker Building & Realty Company	100 00
Atlantic Narrow Fabric Company	200 00
Central Falls Police Relief Association	5 00
Automobile Lining Pneumatic Company	100 00
The Stuart Bastow Company	100 00
Rural Club	5 00
The Bryson Truss Company	100 00
Lazarus & Griess Company	100 00
Sunset Club	5 00
Vennerbeck & Clase Company	100 00
The Perpente-Sisson Company	100 00
The Italian Republican Club	5 00
Pine Grove Club	5 00
Conanicut Island Social Club	5 00
The Providence Auto-Garage Company	100 00
Eddy Realty Company	100 00
Citizens Business Association	5 00
Smith Webbing Company, "Increase"	125 00

Jolt Lubricator Company..................................	100 00
Weekapaug Improvement Society...........................	5 00
The Looff Amusement Company...........................	100 00
Workingman's Protective Association.......................	5 00
Twin City Hospital Association...........................	5 00
Cohen's Hardware & Electric Supply Company...............	100 00
United States Printed Tag Company.......................	100 00
The Westerly Cycle Club.................................	5 00
Victtorio Emmanuli 3rd, Re D'Italio......................	5 00
Plainfield Woolen Company, "Increase"....................	150 00
Measuring Appliance Company............................	100 00
The Automobile Club of Newport.........................	5 00
Providence Jewelry Company.............................	100 00
The Hutchings-Crandall Granite Company..................	100 00
The Providence Evangelization Union of the Methodist Episcopal Church..	5 00
Snow & Farnham Company...............................	100 00
The Bailey Camp Meeting Association of the State of R. I........	5 00
New England Grocery Company...........................	200 00
Montville Woolen Mills & Manufacturing Company...........	100 00
Weekapaug Chapel Society...............................	5 00
McLean-Greene Company.................................	100 00
Cour Lafontaine Forestiers Franco Americains..............	5 00
O'Keefe Company.......................................	100 00
McMullin Holmes Company...............................	100 00
Societa Mutuo Soccorso Vittorio Emmanuele 3rd, of Cranston, R. I..	5 00
The Silver Spring Construction Company...................	700 00
Fidelity Rubber Works...................................	100 00
Westminster Company...................................	100 00
Cercle Josephine.......................................	5 00
The News Publishing Company, "Increase".................	50 00
The Jolly Bachelors....................................	5 00
Empire Literary and Social Club.........................	5 00
Brownell & Field Company, "Increase"....................	165 00
Independent Voters Association of the Third Ward..........	5 00
American Bottling Corporation...........................	100 00
L'Union des Franco Americains de la Nouvelle Angletene........	5 00
H. Midwood's Sons Company..............................	250 00
The Commercial Social Club..............................	5 00
American Druggists Syndicate............................	200 00
The Bowling and Athletic Club...........................	5 00
The Delmont Social Club................................	5 00
C. D. Snow Company....................................	100 00
Manton Patents Company................................	100 00
Olympia Social and Political Club........................	5 00
The Edwin Lowe & Company, Incorporated.................	100 00
Knight & Knight, Incorporated..........................	100 00
R. I. Market Company..................................	100 00

Allen Opera House Company.......	100	00
United Investors Company....	100	00
The Frost Finishing Company....	100	00
Francis Woolen Mills....	100	00
Scituate Gun and Fishing Club....	5	00
The Valley Company....	100	00
La Gloria Citros Fruit Company....	100	00
Richard Roscow Company....	100	00
The Malarine Medical Company....	100	00
East Side Casino Social Club....	5	00
Union Typesetting Company....	100	00
Anchor Webbing Company....	100	00
The Niantic Social Club....	5	00
Bay State Shellac Company....	100	00
Minne-ska Canoe Club....	5	00
Progress Worsted Mills....	100	00
Societa Mutuo Soccorso, Sant 'Antonio No. 706 Dell 'Associazione Ï. C. B. U....	5	00
American Wire and Supply Company....	250	00
The Providence Business Association....	100	00
Pascoag Realty Company....	200	00
Bamford & Smith Company....	100	00
Doleman Optical Company....	100	00
Tillinghast Supply & Machine Company, Incorporated....	100	00
Blackstone Webbing Company, Incorporated....	100	00
Club Pothier....	5	00
Standard Novelty Company....	100	00
Little Pond Company....	100	00
United Land Company....	100	00
Pawtuxet Valley Textile Company....	100	00
The British Club of Rhode Island....	5	00
Woonsocket One Cent Vaudeville Company....	100	00
The William Hughes Company....	100	00
Wellman Lumber Company....	100	00
The F. H. Shoals Company....	100	00
Societa Teanese di Mutuo Soccorso....	5	00
Albert Curry Company....	100	00
The Tierney-Colgan Company....	100	00
The Mary C. Wheeler School Alumnæ Association....	5	00
	$38,217	50

Peddlers' Licenses.

William Walsh, Providence County....	$10	00
Israel Quine, Providence County....	10	00
Louis Lubinsky, Bristol County....	15	00
Charles F. Kopp, Providence County....	30	00
Severe Paquin, City of Providence....	5	00

Maurice Levenson, Providence County........................	10 00
S. Sheron, Providence County...............................	10 00
James Conroy, Kent County.................................	15 00
Herchel Frucht, Providence County.........................	10 00
Joseph Miller, Providence County..........................	10 00
John Burke, Providence County.............................	10 00
Antoine Courier, Kent County..............................	15 00
E. F. Dalton, Providence County...........................	10 00
E. A. Newman, Providence County..........................	10 00
C. E. Post, Providence County.............................	10 00
J. A. Elhatton, Providence County.........................	10 00
J. J. Burns, Providence County............................	10 00
W. E. Durand, Providence County..........................	10 00
Samuel Louis Pearl, Providence County.....................	10 00
H. Yscoss, Providence County..............................	10 00
T. E. Harrigan, Providence County.........................	10 00
R. Fitton, Providence County..............................	10 00
M. Ryan, Providence County...............................	10 00
Abraham Feigen, Providence County........................	10 00
Israel Levin, Providence County............................	10 00
W. Luther Bates, Washington County.......................	15 00
Louis Meisel, Providence County...........................	10 00
Mathew Shaughnessy, State................................	15 00
Francis Abdul, Providence County..........................	10 00
Marks Abrams, Washington County.........................	15 00
Max Lerman, Providence County............................	10 00
Wolf Siegel, Kent County..................................	15 00
Morris Leon, Providence County............................	10 00
Israel Blankstein, Providence County.......................	10 00
Michael Hazzy, Providence County.........................	10 00
M. Goldberg, Providence County...........................	10 00
J. Shapera, Providence County.............................	10 00
Morris Bergel, Providence County..........................	10 00
Michael Corey, Providence County..........................	10 00
George Narcisse, Providence County........................	10 00
Charles Beaulieu, Jewelers, Providence County..............	100 00
Simon Levenson, Providence County........................	10 00
Joseph Falk, Providence County............................	10 00
Edward L. Stone, Providence County.......................	10 00
Peter Moses, Providence County............................	10 00
Mary Ellis, Providence County.............................	10 00
Leon Harootunion, Providence County......................	10 00
Jacob Leon, Providence County.............................	10 00
Mark Glick, State...	15 00
Israel Vorshofsky, Providence County......................	10 00
Harris Davison, Washington County........................	15 00
Israel Lifshitz, Washington County........................	15 00
Sampson Frank, State.....................................	15 00

Louis Berman, Providence County	10	00
Nathan Kahan, Providence County	10	00
Jacob Berkman, Providence County	10	00
Assine Aneyci, Kent County	15	00
Octave Parent, Providence County	10	00
S. Sheron, Providence County	10	00
Severe Paquin, Providence County	10	00
T. Kamen, Providence County	10	00
J. W. Whitley, State	15	00
John Corey, Providence County	10	00
Herschel Frucht, Providence County	10	00
Thomas Hoar, Providence County	10	00
Mary Corey, Providence County	10	00
Mary Joseph, Providence County	10	00
Theofile Laplume, Kent County	15	00
John Burke, Providence County	10	00
Annie Moses, Providence County	10	00
Mary Hanna, Providence County	10	00
James M. Smith, State	15	00
Samuel Lewis Pearl, Providence County	10	00
Lewis Abell, Providence County	10	00
George W. Lewis, Washington County	15	00
Israel Levin, Providence County	30	00
Israel Lipshitz, State	15	00
Louis Meisel, Providence County	10	00
Frank D. Hull, Newport County	15	00
Ernest E. Hampshire, Providence County	10	00
James P. Barry, Bristol County	15	00
Henry Miller, Jewelers, Bristol County	50	00
John Corbridge, Newport County	15	00
Aaron Mack, Providence County	10	00
Harry Sperling, Newport County	15	00
Bernard J. Kilbride, Providence County	10	00
Joseph Coutu, Providence County	10	00
Thomas Conlon, State	15	00
William Conlon, State	15	00
H. Davison, Providence County	10	00
I. Lifshitz, Providence County	10	00
Mike Martinas, Bristol County	15	00
Michael Corey, Providence County	10	00
Robert Campbell, State	15	00
Sam Schwartz, State	15	00
Jacob Berckman, Providence County	30	00
Gabriel Martines, Kent County	15	00
S. Sharon, Providence County	10	00
Abe Sperling, Newport County	15	00
Peter Hanna, Providence County	10	00
David Hivrovitz, Providence County	10	00

Benjamin Fingold, Providence County........................	10 00
Joseph O. Proulx, Providence County........................	10 00
I. J. Benzaquin, State..........................	15 00
Gabriel Martines, Bristol County...........................	15 00
P. Gerzog, Providence County.........................	10 00
Solomon Louis Pearl, Providence County.....................	10 00
Sampson Frank, State............................	15 00
M. Falk, Providence County................................	30 00
Simon Pisetzky, Providence County........................	10 00
Edward White, State...........................	15 00
Michael Huzzy, Providence County............................	10 00
Mary Hubby, Providence County.............................	10 00
Mary Gazelle, Providence County............................	10 00
Aaron Mack, Providence County.............................	30 00
William H. Mellor, Providence County.......................	10 00
Chams Nonglas, Providence County.........................	10 00
Eugene Stevens, Providence County.........................	10 00
John Corey, Providence County............................	10 00
John J. McGee, Providence County.........................	10 00
Harris Charmatz, Providence County.......................	10 00
J. C. Falk, Providence County.............................	10 00
H. Davidson, Providence County...........................	10 00
Morris Brennan, Providence County.........................	10 00
Joseph Cartier, Kent County.............................	15 00
J. Schwatz, Providence County............................	10 00
Peter Corey, Providence County...........................	10 00
Mary David, Providence County...........................	10 00
Sam Davis, Providence County............................	10 00
Bonnie Uderlovitz, Providence County......................	10 00
Abraham Elias, Providence County........................	10 00
Joseph Miller, Providence County..........................	10 00
S. Sharon, Providence County.............................	30 00
Henry Ginsburg, Providence County.........................	10 00
Charles Salzman, Providence County........................	10 00
John Burke, Providence County............................	10 00
Charles McCarty, Providence County.........................	10 00
Samuel Brien, Providence County..........................	10 00
Morris James, Providence County..........................	10 00
Max Mitel, Providence County.............................	10 00
Samuel Schwanenfeld, Providence County.....................	10 00
D. Huroritz, Providence County............................	10 00
Morris Bleistein, Providence County........................	30 00
Hyman Fierstein, State............................	15 00
Louis Sheptwoitch, Providence County......................	10 00
J. Leon, Providence County...............................	10 00
Simon Pistzky, Providence County..........................	10 00

$1,905 00

Auctioneers.

John A. Cowell, Providence	$15 51
Jefferson Aldrich, Woonsocket	4 16
John H. Arnold, Pawtucket	3 99
George S. Baker, Providence	3 29
Arnold A. Manchester, Providence	30 49
Daniel Ahearn, Providence	1 55
Walter F. Crowell, Providence	17 38
George W. Smith, North Smithfield	22
Charles A. Fuller, Richmond	94
Thomas Burlingham, Newport	5 87
Joseph Gilbert, Warwick	1 31
David Frank, Providence	88
Edgar W. Watts, Narragansett	3 29
Charles H. Lawton, Pawtucket	38 33
Henry A. Greene, Providence	7 65
William P. Lewis, New Shoreham	42
Horatio N. Knowles, Narragansett	1 31
Horatio N. Knowles, Narragansett	34
Carlos L. Rogers, Pawtucket	6 30
John B. Carpenter, East Providence	4 96
Walter L. Preston, Providence	21 00
George A. Schuyler, Pawtucket	1 39
James W. Daly, Woonsocket	16 91
Darwin A. Cram, Johnston	26
Reuben A. Wilbur, Cranston	3 78
William C. Tibbitts, Warwick	4 68
Byron L. Kenyon, Hopkinton	25
Thomas O'Brien, Pawtucket	8 44
C. Edward Barney, Providence	28 ·35
Fred E. Horton, Cranston	5 55
George H. Burnham, Providence	15 60
Thomas T. Larkin, Hopkinton	38
Thomas F. Cavanaugh, Woonsocket	1 84
Eugene C. O'Neill, Newport	4 65
James E. Walsh, Providence	12 38
Matthew J. Gallagher, Pawtucket	2 27
Warren Dawley, Richmond	41
Luke Duxbury, Lincoln	3 22
Joseph L. Sanders, Cranston	13 71
Charles C. Conley, Pawtucket	58
William H. Hull, Cranston	57
William H. Hull, Cranston	1 01
Charles A. Phillips, Johnston	1 84
Henry W. Cooke, Providence	24 07
William N. Andrews, Tiverton	4 66
Lyman B. Bosworth, Bristol	04

Clark H. Straight, Bristol......................................	2	37
John J. Corrigan, Burrillville.................................		22
M. J. Gallagher, Pawtucket....................................	1	50
Albert S. Greene, Burrillville.................................	2	54
J. Overton Peckham, Middletown...............................		28
Elijah Anthony, Jamestown....................................		80
Ernest L. Manchester, Little Compton..........................		89
Charles R. Wilbur, Little Compton.............................	2	64
Thomas A. Pingree, Cumberland...............................	8	23
Herbert M. Clarke, Warwick...................................		40
Thomas Burlingham, Newport..................................		88
Henry H. Jencks, Lincoln.....................................	2	15
Norman L. Capwell, West Greenwich...........................		65
Charles P. Baker, Central Falls................................	3	51
Russell L. Slocum, Westerly...................................	1	54
Willard F. Browning, South Kingstown.........................	1	62
Edmund C. Walling, Glocester.................................	4	03
H. C. Budlong, Warwick.......................................	1	05
Joseph Gilbert, Warwick......................................	8	95
Patrick F. Canning, Providence................................	12	36
Daniel Ahearn, Providence....................................	19	46
James H. Hurley, Providence..................................	93	65
Isaac L. Goff, Providence.....................................	19	12
William H. Herrick, Providence...............................	23	02
William C. Tibbitts, Warwick.................................	1	60
Samuel Bernheim, Providence.................................	4	67
Edward J. McCabe, Providence................................	14	58
Theodore Brown, Providence..................................	36	21
John A. Williams, Providence.................................	2	03
Charles A. Clayton, Richmond.................................		07
James F. Freeman, Providence................................	11	40
James R. Jenkins, Providence.................................	32	60
Jefferson Aldrich, Woonsocket.................................	5	07
George W. Smith, North Smithfield............................	4	58
Walter L. Preston, Providence................................	35	89
Samuel B. Hoxie, Charlestown.................................		77
Samuel S. Eldred, South Kingstown............................	8	90
John C. Brown, Warwick......................................		31
Robert L. Walker, Providence.................................	28	04
Charles L. Ellis, Providence..................................	18	22
George L. Robinson, Providence...............................	.5	13
Arnold A. Manchester, Providence.............................	33	34
Edwin Draper, Providence....................................	5	75
Edwin Draper, Providence....................................	22	30
Joseph W. Lewis, Providence..................................	107	84
Coomer S. Ford, Scituate.....................................	4	85
Byron L. Kenyon, Hopkinton..................................	1	62
George S. Baker, Providence..................................	5	84

Joseph A. Latham, Cranston		12
Joseph A. Latham, Cranston	30	89
Joseph M. Provencher, Jr., Woonsocket		18
Charles O. Latham, Cranston	1	26
David Frank, Providence	3	28
Thomas F. Cavanaugh, Woonsocket	2	81
Abraham Colitz, Woonsocket	1	20
John B. McGuinness, Providence	11	23
Charles A. Fuller, Richmond		21
C. Edward Barney, Providence	36	07
John B. Carpenter, East Providence	10	98
William A. Baggott, Providence	7	39
George H. Burnham, Providence	13	41
Thomas T. Larkin, Hopkinton	1	47
Henry A. Shippee, Warwick	2	30
William A. Baggott, Providence		49
Herbert C. Calef, Johnston	4	91
Horatio N. Knowles, Narragansett	79	77
Robert H. Walker, Scituate		29
John H. Arnold, Pawtucket	53	68
C. H. Straight, Bristol	2	31
Charles H. Lawton, Pawtucket	6	71
Joseph Perkins, Jr., Warwick		05
Albert S. Greene, Burrillville	1	81
J. Overton Peckham, Middletown	1	41
Henry C. Budlong, Warwick		26
Matthew J. Gallagher, Pawtucket	6	86
Patrick J. McCarthy, Providence		88
Thomas A. Pingree, Cumberland	7	66
Henry A. Shippee, Warwick		13
Levi Staples, Barrington		85
Stephen T. Arnold, East Greenwich	4	79
Henry F. True, Hopkinton		77
Richard LeBaron Bowen, East Providence		14
Charles P. Baker, Central Falls	6	40
Henry H. Franklin, Cumberland		78
Charles L. Hazard, East Providence	14	08
Herman G. Tucker, Foster	1	32
Willard F. Browning, South Kingstown		28
Russell L. Slocum, Westerly	3	30
Levi Staples, Barrington		16
William H. Herrick, Providence	10	77
Patrick F. Canning, Providence	18	93
Frank W. Sherman, North Kingstown		71
James R. Jenkins, Providence	13.59	
James A. Hurley, Providence	244	12
Charles L. Ellis, Providence	24	40
C. Edward Barney, Providence	20	90

James Anthony, Middletown...................................... 10 54
George S. Baker, Providence.................................... 10 30
James F. Freeman, Providence.................................. 9 54
Richard A. Hurley, Providence................................. 24
Daniel Ahearn, Providence..................................... 70
Robert L. Walker, Providence.................................. 11 66

$1,628 79

Commercial Fertilizers.

Swift's Lowell Fertilizer Company—
    Swift's Lowell Bone Fertilizer............................ $18 00
    Swift's Lowell Potato Phosphate......................... 18 00
    Swift's Lowell Animal Brand.............................. 18 00
    Swift's Lowell Potato Manure............................ 18 00
John Joynt—
    Wood Ashes... 12 00
Russia Cement Company—
    Essex R. I. Special for Potatoes, Roots, and Vegetables.... 18 00
    Essex Complete Manure for Potatoes, Roots, and Vegetables 18 00
    Essex Complete Manure for Corn, Grain, and Grass........ 18 00
    Essex Market Garden and Potato Fertilizer............... 18 00
    Essex XXX Fish and Potash.............................. 18 00
F. R. Lalor—
    Wood Ashes... 12 00
The American Agricultural Chemical Company—
    Bradley's Complete Manure for Potatoes and Vegetables.... 18 00
    Bradley's Complete Manure for Top-dressing, Grass, and
        Grain.. 18 00
    Bradley's Complete Manure for Corn and Grain........... 18 00
    Bradley's English Lawn Fertilizer....................... 18 00
    Bradley's X. L. Superphosphate of Lime................. 18 00
    Bradley's Potato Manure................................ 18 00
    Bradley's Corn Phosphate............................... 18 00
    Bradley's Eclipse Phosphate............................ 18 00
    Bradley's Niagara Phosphate............................ 18 00
    Bradley's Potato Fertilizer............................. 18 00
    Baker's A. A. Ammoniated Superphosphate.............. 18 00
    Baker's Complete Potato Manure........................ 18 00
    Brightman's Fish and Potash............................ 18 00
    Church's Fish and Potash............................... 18 00
    Darling's Blood, Bone, and Potash...................... 18 00
    Darling's Potato and Root Crop Manure................. 18 00
    Darling's Lawn and Garden Fertilizer................... 18 00
    Darling's Animal Fertilizer............................. 18 00
    Darling's General Fertilizer............................ 18 00
    Quinnipiac Market Garden Manure...................... 18 00
    Quinnipiac Phosphate.................................. 18 00

The American Agricultural Chemical Company—

Quinnipiac Potato Manure..............................	18 00
Quinnipiac Potato Phosphate..........................	18 00
Quinnipiac Corn Manure..............................	18 00
Quinnipiac Pequot Fish and Potash....................	18 00
Quinnipiac Climax Phosphate..........................	18 00
Williams & Clark High Grade Special..................	18 00
Williams & Clark Ammoniated Bone Superphosphate......	18 00
Williams & Clark Corn Phosphate......................	18 00
Williams & Clark Potato Phosphate....................	18 00
Williams & Clark Potato Manure......................	18 00
Williams & Clark Royal Bone Phosphate................	18 00
Grass and Lawn Top Dressing..........................	18 00
Macomber Formula....................................	18 00
Fine Ground Bone....................................	12 00
Nitrate of Soda.....................................	6 00
Muriate of Potash...................................	6 00
Kainit...	6 00
Plain Superphosphate................................	6 00

The Rogers & Hubbard Company—

Hubbard's Oats and Top Dressing Fertilizer.............	18 00
Hubbard's Grass and Grain Fertilizer..................	18 00
Hubbard's Soluble Corn Fertilizer.....................	18 00
Hubbard's Soluble Potato Fertilizer...................	18 00
Hubbard's All Soils, All Crops Fertilizer..............	18 00
Hubbard's Corn Phosphate............................	18 00
Hubbard's Potato Phosphate..........................	18 00
Hubbard's R. K. Bone Flour..........................	12 00
Hubbard's Strictly Pure Fine Bone....................	12 00
Hubbard's Market Garden Phosphate...................	18 00

E. Frank Coe Company—

E. Frank Coe's High Grade Ammoniated Bone Superphosphate...	18 00
E. Frank Coe's Celebrated Special Potato Fertilizer.........	18 00
E. Frank Coe's Columbian Potato Fertilizer..............	18 00
E. Frank Coe's XXV Ammoniated Bone Phosphate........	18 00

The Mitchell Fertilizer Company—

Mitchell's Vegetable Fertilizer........................	18 00
Mitchell's Special Fertilizer..........................	18 00

National Fertilizer Company—

Chittenden's Market Garden...........................	18 00
Chittenden's Fish and Potash.........................	18 00
Chittenden's Ammoniated Bone Phosphate..............	18 00
Chittenden's Complete Fertilizer......................	18 00

T. H. Frauley—

Canada Hard Wood Unleached Ashes...................	12 00

Parmenter & Polsey Fertilizer Company—

Plymouth Rock Brand................................	18 00

Parmenter & Polsey Fertilizer Company—

Star Brand	18 00
Special Potato	18 00
P. & P. Potato	18 00
Ground Bone	12 00
Nitrate of Soda	6 00
Muriate of Potash	6 00
Acid Phosphate	6 00

Bowker Fertilizer Company—

Stockbridge Potato Manure	18 00
Stockbridge Corn and Grain Manure	18 00
Stockbridge Top Dressing	18 00
Bowker's Early Potato Manure	18 00
Bowker's Potato and Vegetable Fertilizer	18 00
Bowker's Potato and Vegetable Phosphate	18 00
Bowker's R. I. Potato Manure	18 00
Bowker's Hill and Drill Phosphate	18 00
Bowker's Farm and Garden Phosphate	18 00
Bowker's Fish and Potash, "D" Brand	18 00
Anthony's Formula B	18 00
Bowker's Sure Crop Phosphate	18 00
Bowker's Bristol Fish and Potash	18 00
Bowker's Gloucester Fish and Potash	18 00
Canada Hardwood Ashes	12 00
Nitrate of Soda	6 00
Muriate of Potash	6 00
Bowker's Fresh Ground Bone	12 00
Bowker's Corn Phosphate	18 00
Bowker's Lawn and Garden Dressing	18 00

Berkshire Fertilizer Company—

Complete Fertilizer	18 00
Potato and Vegetable Phosphate	18 00

Mason Manufacturing Company—

Tankage	12 00

Wilcox Fertilizer Works—

Wilcox Potato, Onion, and Vegetable Manure	18 00
Wilcox Potato Fertilizer	18 00
Wilcox C. B. Superphosphate	18 00
Wilcox Special Superphosphate	18 00
Wilcox Fish and Potash	18 00
Wilcox Grass Fertilizer	18 00
Wilcox Nitrate of Soda	6 00
Wilcox Muriate of Potash	6 00
Wilcox Pure Ground Bone	12 00

M. L. Shoemaker & Company, Ltd.—

"Swift-Sure" Super Phosphate for General Use	18 00
"Swift-Sure" Super Phosphate for Potatoes	18 00
"Swift-Sure" Guano for Truck, Corn, and Onions	18 00

M. L. Shoemaker & Company, Ltd.—
  "Swift-Sure" Bone Meal.................................   12 00
The Armour Fertilizer Company—
  Blood, Bone, and Potash..............................   18 00
  High Grade Potato....................................   18 00
  All Soluble..   18 00
  Market Garden..   18 00
  Corn King..   18 00
  Complete Potato......................................   18 00
  Ammoniated Bone with Potash.........................   18 00
The Rogers Manufacturing Company—
  Potato and Vegetable Fertilizer......................   18 00
Sanderson Fertilizer & Chemical Company—
  Sanderson's Formula A................................   18 00
  Sanderson's Potato Manure............................   18 00
  Sanderson's Corn Superphosphate......................   18 00
  Niantic Bone, Fish, and Potash.......................   18 00
C. M. Shay Fertilizer Company—
  Shay's Potato Manure.................................   18 00
Andrews & Spelman—
  Canada Hard Wood Ashes...............................   12 00
Wilcox Fertilizer Works—
  Acid Phosphate.......................................   6 00
American Agricultural Chemical Company. (M. E. Wheeler &
  Company, Branch.)—
  Corn Special...   18 00
Potato Manure..   18 00
Superior Truck...   18 00
Bowker Fertilizer Company—
  Market Garden..   18 00
The Wunsch Manufacturing Company—
  Tankage..   12 00
Isaac L. Sherman—
  Wilcox's Portsmouth Grange, Formula A...............   18 00
J. A. Woodmansee—
  Acid Phosphate.......................................   6 00
Sanderson Fertilizer & Chemical Company—
  Sanderson's Special with 10 per cent. Potash.........   18 00
  Walker's Complete Phosphate..........................   18 00
  Walker's High Grade Fertilizer.......................   18 00
James L. Reynolds—
  Florists, High Grade Blood and Bone..................   12 00
Smith Agricultural Chemical Company—
  General Crop and Fish Guano..........................   18 00
The Armour Fertilizer Works—
  Grain Grower...   18 00
  Bone Meal..   12 00
  Ammoniated Bone......................................   18 00

Smith Agricultural Chemical Company—
Ammoniated Bone and Potash......................... 18 00
William B. Scott & Company—
Bone.. 12 00
The National Fertilizer Company—
Chittenden's Fine Ground Bone...................... 12 00
Chittenden's Complete Grain 18 00
Chittenden's Complete Grass....................... 18 00

$2,436 00

Supreme Courts.

Costs... $6,226 20
Jurors.. 3,668 50
Officers.. 143 30
Witnesses....................................... 344 50
Fines... 2,733 85
Incidentals..................................... 59 21

$13,175 56

First Judicial District Court.

Entries and Executions.................................. $361 45
Writs... 28 00
Fines... 1,125 00
Costs... 1,076 85
Court Fees in Town Cases............................... 686 55

$3,277 85

Second Judicial District Court.

Entries and Executions.................................. $27 60
Writs... 4 50
Fines... 85 00
Costs... 297 15
Court Fees in Town Cases............................... 67 70

$481 95

Third Judicial District Court.

Entries and Executions.................................. $37 30
Writs... 7 70
Fines... 119 00
Costs... 188 00
Court Fees in Town Cases............................... 151 70

$503 70

Fourth Judicial District Court.

Entries and Executions	$117 75
Writs	9 90
Fines	216 00
Costs	490 35
Court Fees in Town Cases	155 00
	$989 00

Fifth Judicial District Court.

Entries and Executions	$57 60
Writs	9 45
Fines	406 00
Costs	708 65
Court Fees in Town Cases	85 65
	$1,267 35

Sixth Judicial District Court.

Entries and Executions	$3,391 55
Writs	480 10
Fines	6,830 00
Costs	3,587 30
Court Fees in Town Cases	34 05
	$14,323 00

Seventh Judicial District Court.

Entries and Executions	$100 00
Writs	1 55
Fines	238 00
Costs	280 90
Court Fees in Town Cases	329 80
	$950 25

Eighth Judicial District Court.

Entries and Executions	$104 90
Writs	4 10
Fines	380 00
Costs	443 05
Court Fees in Town Cases	94 00
	$1,026 05

Ninth Judicial District Court.

Entries and Executions......................................	$24 45
Writs..	3 10
Fines..	63 00
Costs..	68 80
Court Fees in Town Cases....................................	50 80
	$210 15

Tenth Judicial District Court.

Entries and Executions......................................	$331 75
Writs..	31 55
Fines..	562 00
Costs..	537 30
Court Fees in Town Cases....................................	590 05
	$2,052 65

Eleventh Judicial District Court.

Entries and Executions......................................	$223 60
Writs..	5 90
Fines..	626 40
Costs..	581 50
Court Fees in Town Cases....................................	317 75
	$1,755 15

Twelfth Judicial District Court.

Entries and Executions......................................	$247 80
Writs..	14 25
Fines..	381 00
Costs..	244 10
Court Fees in Town Cases....................................	69 30
	$956 45

Jailers.

James H. Eastman, Superintendent, State Institutions..........	$1,221 99
Andrew J. Wilcox, Providence County.........................	4,902 98
Hugh N. Gifford, Newport County.............................	19 80
Frank P. King, Newport County...............................	88 60
James Anthony, Sheriff, Newport County......................	5 30
John R. Wilcox, Washington County...........................	38 90
	$6,277 57

Civil Commissions.

Charles P. Bennett, Secretary of State..........................	$602 00
Hunter C. White, Sheriff, Providence County...................	1,796 00
James Anthony, Sheriff, Newport County......................	196 00
John R. Wilcox, Sheriff, Washington County..................	176 00
Michael B. Lynch, Sheriff, Kent County.....................	112 00
Philo V. Cady, Sheriff, Bristol County.........................	56 00
	$2,938 00

Dividends on the School Fund.

Interest on Town of Cranston Bonds..........................	$40 00
Interest on Town of East Providence Bonds...................	920 00
Interest on Town of Johnston Bonds....:.....................	640 00
Interest on Town of Bristol Bonds............................	980 00
Interest on Town of Warren Bonds...........................	800 00
Interest on City of Woonsocket Bonds........................	120 00
Interest on Town of Lincoln Bonds...........................	4,600 00
Dividend, National Bank of Commerce........................	1,015 00
Interest, call account, Industrial Trust Company...............	16 37
	$9,131 37

Interest on Deposit of the Revenue.

Rhode Island Hospital Trust Company........................	$1,756 09
Industrial Trust Company...................................	1,401 67
	$3,157 76

National Home for Disabled Volunteer Soldiers.

Received from the U. S. Treasury Department..................	$13,374 84

State Institutions in Cranston.

Charles H. Peckham, Secretary Board of State Charities and Corrections...	$54,352 41

State Home and School.

R. B. Risk, Superintendent....................................	$211 54
Dr. W. A. Risk, Superintendent...............................	388 91
	$600 45

Commissioners of Shell Fisheries.

Received from James C. Collins, Clerk........................	$47,087 26

General Laws.

Charles P. Bennett, Secretary of State......................... $66 00

Public Laws.

Charles P. Bennett, Secretary of State......................... $118 45

Rhode Island Reports.

Charles P. Bennett, Secretary of State......................... $1,315 00

Acts and Resolves.

Charles P. Bennett, Secretary of State......................... $16 25

Automobile and Motor Cycle Licenses.

Charles P. Bennett, Secretary of State......................... $1,684 00

Proceeds from Sales at Camp Ground R. I. M.

Received of W. Howard Walker, Quartermaster-General.......... $260 00

Firemen's Relief Fund.

Received of Frederic W. Cady, Treasurer...................... $1,413 53

Military and Naval Expenses, War with Spain.

Received from U. S. Government............................. $6,907 95

Notes.

Rhode Island Hospital Trust Company.........................	$50,000 00
Commissioners of Sinking Fund.............................	45,000 00
	$95,000 00

Steam and Street Railroads, on Account of Salary and Expenses of Railroad Commissioner.

New York, New Haven & Hartford Railroad...................	$494 42
Providence & Worcester......................................	121 78
Boston & Providence..	41 99
Providence & Springfield....................................	89 89
Newport & Wickford R. R. & S. B. Co......................	28 22
Narragansett Pier..	40 09
Wood River Branch...	21 28
Old Colony..	73 11

Providence, Warren & Bristol	50	12
New England	101	92
Pawtuxet Valley	17	88
Rhode Island & Massachusetts	19	28
Moshassuck Valley	24	01
Woonsocket & Pascoag	27	47
Union Railroad	614	11
Pawtucket Street Railway	88	83
Woonsocket Street Railway	80	03
Pawcatuck Valley Street Railway	23	84
Newport & Fall River Street Railway	50	74
Old Colony Street Railway	55	18
Sea View Railroad	68	35
Newport & Providence Railway	33	59
Rhode Island Suburban Railway	308	78
Providence & Danielson Railway	91	28
The Rhode Island Co	1,397	47
Columbian Street Railway	36	34
	$4,000	00

Tax on Street Railway Companies.

The Rhode Island Company and leased roads	$56,345	01
Old Colony Street Railway Company	1,377	80
Woonsocket Street Railway Company	1,025	68
Providence & Danielson Railway Company	843	07
Sea View Railroad Company	636	14
Pawcatuck Valley Street Railway Company	250	42
	$60,478	12

Tax on Express Companies.

Adams Express Company	$523	64
New York & Boston Despatch Express Company	7	50
	$531	14

Tax on Telephone Companies.

Providence Telephone Company	$7,304	85
Westerly Automatic Telephone Company	53	19
Hope Valley Clark Automatic Telephone Company	11	47
American Telephone & Telegraph Company	46	13
The Southern Massachusetts Telephone Company	66	90
Westerly Automatic Telephone Company	102	12
The Coventry Telephone Company	15	65
	$7,600	31

Tax on Telegraph Companies.

Western Union Telegraph Company........................	$812 88
Postal Telegraph & Cable Company........................	10 15
	$823 03

Construction and Improvement of State Highways.

Received of Town Treasurer, Tiverton.....................	$421 60
Received of Town Treasurer, Narragansett.................	700 00
Received of Town Treasurer, Bristol......................	934 28
Received of Town Treasurer, Coventry.....................	3,757 40
Received of T. D. Babcock, for Town of Westerly..........	250 00
Received of Town Treasurer, Smithfield...................	800 00
Received of Town Treasurer, Richmond....................	342 93
	$7,206 21

Rent of Old Normal School Building.

William O. Blanding, Treasurer, R. I. College of Pharmacy and Allied Sciences..	$680 00

Tuition, Rhode Island Normal School.

Received of City of Providence, quarter ending January 17.......	$1,860 36
Received of City of Providence, quarter ending April 14..........	1,894 17
Received of City of Providence, quarter ending June 30..........	1,938 38
	$5,692 91

State Sanatorium for Consumptives.

George F. Whitford, Treasurer............................	$500 02

Miscellaneous.

Received of Sanford E. Kinnecom, for beer barrels, etc..........	$15 00
Received of Charles S. Bush & Company, for duplicate check.....	8 20
Received of Orrin E. Huntley, for rent of Infantry Hall, Pawtucket .	5 00
Received of Providence Gas Company, for rebate on bills of 1904....	97 72
Conscience Fund...	40 00
Received of Chas. P. Bennett, Secretary of State, for rebate of express charges..	40
Received of John Ogden, Town Treasurer, for 12 days' interest on State tax..	3 19
Received of S. R. Richmond, Town Treasurer, for 27 days' interest on State tax..	7 21
Received of Harbor Commissioners, for the sale of old wreck......	10 00
Received of Charles M. Arnold, Clerk, for sales of bottles, jugs, etc...	2 90

Received of Walter A. Read, General Treasurer, for sale of postage stamps......	2	78
Received of George H. Utter, Governor......	509	66
Received of Col. Zenas W. Bliss, return premiums on policies cancelled......	4	16
Received of Walter R. Wightman, Agent, for board of inmates at Butler Asylum......	143	61
Received for court charges in Sixth District Court......	30	60
Received for interest on bank account......	1	30
Received of Almanza J. Roset, Town Treasurer, for 72 days' interest on State tax......	23	10
Received of Charles P. Bennett, Secretary of State, for Sale of Court and Practice Act......	6	25
Received for Portsmouth Records......	4	00
Received for prepaid postage......	1	36
Received of Edwin G. Penniman, Treasurer of Louisiana Purchase Exposition Commission......	2,738	03
	$3,654	47

PAYMENTS IN DETAIL.

A.

Salaries.

Lucius F. C. Garvin, Governor......	$24	20
George H. Utter, Governor......	2,975	80
George H. Utter, Lieutenant-Governor......	4	03
Frederick H. Jackson, Lieutenant-Governor......	495	97
Charles P. Bennett, Secretary of State......	3,500	00
Charles F. Stearns, Attorney-General......	36	29
William B. Greenough, Attorney-General......	4,463	71
Walter A. Read, General Treasurer......	2,500	00
Charles C. Gray, State Auditor and Insurance Commissioner......	2,500	00
William B. Greenough, Assistant Attorney-General......	20	16
James C. Collins, Jr., Assistant Attorney-General......	2,479	84
Thomas B. Stockwell, Commissioner of Public Schools......	1,750	00
Walter E. Ranger, Commissioner of Public Schools......	1,250	00
Henry E. Tiepke, Commissioner of Industrial Statistics......	166	67
George H. Webb, Commissioner of Industrial Statistics......	1,833	33
Gideon E. Spencer, Secretary, State Board Soldiers' Relief......	2,000	00
Gardner T. Swarts, Secretary, State Board of Health......	1,700	00
Ella M. Rogers, Secretary of the Supreme Court......	1,500	00
Edward C. Stiness, Reporter of Decisions of Supreme Court......	1,200	00
J. Harry Bongartz, Librarian of Law Library......	1,200	00
J. Ellery Hudson, Factory Inspector......	1,896	50
Helen M. Jencks, Factory Inspector......	1,500	00

Joseph Roy, Factory Inspector........................... .....   1,165 32
Edward L. Freeman, Railroad Commissioner.............. ... .   2,500 00
Joseph W. Freeman, Deputy Railroad Commissioner.............   500 00
Frederic M. Sackett, Adjutant-General........................   1,200 00
W. Howard Walker, Quartermaster-General....................   1,000 00
John H. Wetherell, Assistant Adjutant-General.................   250 00
Arthur V. Warfield, Assistant Adjutant-General, "B. R. I. M.."....   250 00
J. Herbert Shedd, Harbor Commissioner......................   600 00
Alfred W. Kenyon, Harbor Commissioner.....................   600 00
Henry T. Root, Harbor Commissioner........................   600 00
J. Fred Parker, Clerk of the Secretary of State..............   2,000 00
Charles C. Clark, Clerk of the General Treasurer.................   1,500 00
Charles M. Arnold, Clerk of the State Auditor................   2,000 00
Grace F. Underwood, Clerk of the State Auditor.................   750 00
Esther F. Rebholtz, Clerk of the State Auditor.................   600 00
Felix Hebert, Clerk of the Insurance Commissioner.............   1,500 00
Luly M. Coggeshall, Clerk of the Commissioner of Public Schools..   750 00
Walter C. Simmons, Commissioner of Dams and Reservoirs.......   1,000 00
James W. Munroe, Crier of Courts, Providence County...........   429 03
Frederick W. Wing, Crier of Supreme Court..................   171 24
George H. Pettis, State Sealer of Weights and Measures...........   500 00
Frank E. Holden, State Returning Board......................   427 78
C. Clarence Maxson, State Returning Board..................   72 22
George R. Lawton, State Returning Board....................   500 00
Charles H. Handy, State Returning Board....................   500 00
Arthur S. Fitz, State Returning Board......................   500 00
Thomas J. Dorney, State Returning Board....................   500 00
Charles Matteson, Ex-Chief Justice of the Supreme Court.........   5,500 00
John H. Stiness, Ex-Chief Justice of the Supreme Court..........   5,500 00
P. E. Tillinghast, Chief Justice of the Supreme Court.............   605 65
P. E. Tillinghast, Ex-Chief Justice of the Supreme Court.........   2,144 35
George A. Wilbur, Associate Justice of the Supreme Court.........   2,715 06
George A. Wilbur, Ex-Justice of the Supreme Court.............   2,284 94
William W. Douglas, Associate Justice of the Supreme Court......   2,919 61
William W. Douglas, Chief Justice of the Supreme Court.........   2,741 94
Edward C. Dubois, Associate Justice of the Supreme Court.......   5,228 50
John T. Blodgett, Associate Justice of the Supreme Court........   5,228 50
Clarke H. Johnson, Associate Justice of the Supreme Court.......   5,228 50
C. Frank Parkhurst, Associate Justice of the Supreme Court......   4,424 42
William H. Sweetland, Presiding Justice, Superior Court.........   2,520 84
Willard B. Tanner, Associate Justice, Superior Court............   2,291 66
Darius Baker, Associate Justice, Superior Court................   2,291 66
Charles F. Stearns, Associate Justice, Superior Court...........   2,291 66
Charles C. Mumford, Associate Justice, Superior Court..........   2,291 66
George T. Brown, Associate Justice, Superior Court.............   2,291 66
Bertram S. Blaisdell, Clerk, Appellate Division, Supreme Court,
    Providence County.......................................   1,357 53
Bertram S. Blaisdell, Clerk of Supreme Court..................   1,142 47

David B. Pike, Assistant Clerk, Appellate Division, Supreme Court,
  Providence County.. 977 42
David B. Pike, Assistant Clerk of Supreme Court................. 822 58
Harry M. Paine, Additional Assistant Clerk, Appellate Division,
  Supreme Court, Providence County......................... 543 01
Harry M. Paine, Assistant Clerk, Supreme Court, Providence
  County.. 685 49
Walter S. Reynolds, Clerk, Common Pleas Division, Supreme Court.
  Providence County....................................... 1,357 53
Walter S. Reynolds, Clerk, Superior Court, Providence and Bristol
  County.. 1,142 47
Horace G. Bissell, Assistant Clerk, Common Pleas Division, Supreme
  Court, Providence County................................ 977 42
Horace G. Bissell, Assistant Clerk, Superior Court, Providence and
  Bristol County.. 822 58
G. Frederick Frost, Assistant Clerk, Superior Court, Providence and
  Bristol County.. 687 50
Charles C. Gilbert, Assistant Clerk, Superior Court, Providence and
  Bristol County.. 595 84
Oscar L. Heltzen, Assistant Clerk, Superior Court, Providence and
  Bristol County.. 550 00
Robert C. Root, Assistant Clerk, Superior Court, Providence and
  Bristol County.. 550 00
Henry W. Stiness, Assistant Clerk, Superior Court, Providence and
  Bristol County.. 550 00
Charles E. Harvey, Clerk, Appellate and Common Pleas Division,
  Supreme Court, Newport County.......................... 977 42
Charles E. Harvey, Clerk, Superior Court, Newport County....... 822 58
Henry M. Thompson, Clerk, Common Pleas Division, Supreme
  Court, Bristol County................................... 325 81
Henry M. Thompson, Assistant Clerk, Superior Court, Providence
  and Bristol County...................................... 274 19
Henry A. Thomas, Clerk, Common Pleas Division, Supreme Court,
  Kent County.. 651 61
Henry A. Thomas, Clerk, Superior Court, Kent County.......... 548 39
William H. Caswell, Clerk, Appellate and Common Pleas Division,
  Supreme Court, Washington County....................... 814 52
William H. Caswell, Clerk, Superior Court, Washington County..... 548 39
Darius Baker, Justice, District Court, First Judicial District........ 433 33
Robert M. Franklin, Justice, District Court, First Judicial District.. 761 29
George H. Kelley, Clerk, District Court, First Judicial District...... 1,000 00
Nathan B. Lewis, Justice, District Court, Second Judicial District.... 1,000 00
Thomas J. Peirce, Clerk, District Court, Second Judicial District... 377 42
John W. Sweeney, Justice, District Court, Third Judicial District.... 91 67
Oliver H. Williams, Justice, District Court, Third Judicial District.. 1,008 33
Edward G. Cundall, Clerk, District Court, Third Judicial District.... 83 33
Elmer J. Rathbun, Justice, District Court, Fourth Judicial District.. 1,200 00
George A. Loomis, Clerk, District Court, Fourth Judicial District.. 800 00

Orrin L. Bosworth, Justice, District Court, Fifth Judicial District...	1,000 00
Arthur W. Joyce, Clerk, District Court, Fifth Judicial District.....	511 83
William H. Sweetland, Justice, District Court, Sixth Judicial District......	1,440 86
Frederick Rueckert, Justice, District Court, Sixth Judicial District..	2,559 14
Frederick Rueckert, Clerk, District Court, Sixth Judicial District....	900 53
Christopher M. Lee, Clerk, District Court, Sixth Judicial District.....	1,592 75
George N. Bliss, Justice, District Court, Seventh Judicial District....	1,000 00
William C. Bliss, Clerk, District Court, Seventh Judicial District....	600 00
Henry A. Palmer, Justice, District Court, Eighth Judicial District...	1,200 00
Willis S. Knowles, Clerk, District Court, Eighth Judicial District..	1,000 00
James Harris, Justice, District Court, Ninth Judicial District......	1,000 00
Frank H. Potter, Clerk, District Court, Ninth Judicial District......	350 00
Lellan J. Tuck, Justice, District Court, Tenth Judicial District......	1,200 00
Joseph McDonald, Clerk, District Court, Tenth Judicial District...	83 33
Robert S. Emerson, Clerk, District Court, Tenth Judicial District....	916 67
Ambrose Choquet, Justice, District Court, Eleventh Judicial District......	1,133 33
Horace A. Follett, Clerk, District Court, Eleventh Judicial District..	1,000 00
Ambrose Feely, Justice, District Court, Twelfth Judicial District..	1,200 00
Charles M. Arnold, Clerk, District Court, Twelfth Judicial District	800 00
Hunter C. White, Sheriff, Providence County..................	5,000 00
James Anthony, Sheriff, Newport County......................	741 66
Philo V. Cady, Sheriff, Bristol County........................	683 33
Michael B. Lynch, Sheriff, Kent County......................	683 33
John R. Wilcox, Sheriff, Washington County...................	683 33
John H. Northup, Commissioner of Shell Fisheries..............	500 00
Philip H. Wilbour, Commissioner of Shell Fisheries..............	500 00
James M. Wright, Commissioner of Shell Fisheries..............	500 00
Samuel B. Hoxie, Jr., Commissioner of Shell Fisheries...........	166 67
William T. Lewis, Jr., Commissioner of Shell Fisheries...........	166 67
George W. Hoxie, Commissioner of Shell Fisheries..............	330 64
Herbert M. Gardiner, Commissioner of Shell Fisheries...........	330 64
Frederick E. Perkins, State Board of Public Roads..............	347 22
Robert B. Treat, State Board of Public Roads..................	347 22
John H. Edwards, State Board of Public Roads.................	347 22
John F. Richmond, State Board of Public Roads................	347 22
William C. Peckham, State Board of Public Roads..............	347 22
	$171,853 63

Clerks of the General Assembly.

David J. White, Clerk, Senate................................	$1,000 00
Raymond G. Mowry, Reading Clerk, House of Representatives....	1,000 00
Charles H. Howland, Recording Clerk, House of Representatives..	1,000 00
	$3,000 00

Clerks of Committees of the General Assembly.

John W. Sweeney, Senate, Judiciary............................	$800 00
Arthur A. Rhodes, House, Judiciary...........................	800 00
Frederic A. Greene, Senate, Finance.........................	800 00
James J. Nolan, House, Finance..............................	800 00
Arthur W. Joyce, Senate, Corporations......................	800 00
John Ogden, House, Corporations............................	800 00
Clifford S. Tower, Senate, Education........................	500 00
Thomas Allen, House, Education..............................	500 00
Herbert A. Blake, Senate, Special Legislation..............	500 00
Frederick A. Jones, House, Special Legislation............	500 00
William R. Champlin, Senate, Fisheries....................	500 00
Wilbur A. Scott, Public Institutions........................	500 00
John D. Turner, Joint Committee, Accounts and Claims.........	500 00
Lester E. Dodge, Engrossing Clerk..........................	600 00
	$8,900 00

Executive Secretary.

Robert Grieve...	$9 68
Richard W. Jennings..	1,190 32
	$1,200 00

State Librarian.

Herbert O. Brigham...	$1,127 95

State Registrar.

Gardner T. Swarts..	$1,000 00

Additional Clerk Hire, Secretary of State.

Walter H. Bullard..	$1,200 00

Clerical Assistance Rendered Secretary of State.

Ernest L. Sprague..	$1,133 33

Clerk of the Attorney-General.

Alice C. Burnham...	$500 00

Additional Clerical Assistance, General Treasurer.

Hattie M. Fletcher...	$750 00
Leverett C. Stevens..	106 00
	$856 00

Clerical Assistance, Adjutant-General.

Bertha Allen..	$540 00
Ellery E. Hudson...	420 00
Alice A. Griffin..	540 00
	$1,500 00

Clerical Assistance, Quartermaster-General.

Blanche Johnson...	$500 00
Thomas Kieran...	500 00
	$1,000 00

Additional Clerical Assistance, Insurance Commissioner.

Minnie H. Davenport...	$592 00
Louise Bowen..	480 00
Julia B. A. Rich...	528 00
	$1,600 00

Clerk, Commissioners of Shell Fisheries.

James C. Collins...	$1,319 89

Secretary, Commissioners of Inland Fisheries.

William P. Morton..	$600 00

Secretary of the State Returning Board.

Richard W. Jennings....:....................................	$1,000 00

Clerical Assistance, State Returning Board.

Mary E. Jackson...	$100 00
Thomas Allen..	75 00
Robert B. Healy...	75 00
Arthur V. Warfield..	75 00
William A. Heathman...	75 00
Oscar A. Carleton...	10 00
	$410 00

Clerical Assistance, First District Court.

Laura G. Tilley...	$300 00

Clerical Assistance, Sixth District Court.

George F. Mackinnon..	$1,000 00
George L. Smith..	458 34
Mabel L. Smith...	41 66
	$1,500 00

Clerical Assistance, Assistant Adjutant-General, B. R. I. M.

Arthur V. Warfield...	$500 00

Clerical Assistance for Clerk, Common Pleas Division, Supreme Court, Providence County.

G. Frederick Frost..	$556 40
Charles C. Gilbert..	556 40
Leonard W. Horton...	912 50
	$2,025 30

Clerical Assistance for Clerk, Appellate and Common Pleas Division, Supreme Court, Newport County.

Sadie A. Harvey..	$162 90

Clerical Assistance for Clerk, Superior Court, Newport County.

Sadie A. Harvey..	$62 10
Sydney D. Harvey..	75 00
	$137 10

Messengers, New State House.

Joseph Mullen...	$1,000 00
Charles C. Gray, Jr..	1,000 00
	$2,000 00

Care of Sixth Judicial District Court House.

John J. Butler...	$900 00
Charles F. Snell...	600 00
	$1,500 00

Care, Providence County Court House.

George F. Sweet...	$583 31
Hugh F. McCusker...	960 00
Albert H. Warner..	906 65

Grace W. Slocum	720	00
George Atwood	720	00
John A. Slocum	477	67
James Boyle	410	00
Jane Sharp	360	00
Cephas N. Johnson	325	00
Henry Dean	240	00
Jacob Johnson	225	62
Jessey M. Cresser	175	00
Charles Boyle	185	83
Helena E. McKenzie	145	00
Benjamin Cain	61	33
William Wood	74	16
Leon P. Brown	42	16
Clive P. Brown	21	00
	$6,632	**73**

Care, Newport County Court House.

Robert E. Brooks	$533	33

Care, Woonsocket Court House.

Thomas Higginbottom	$600	00
George H. Prue	600	00
	$1,200	**00**

Janitor, Bristol County Court House.

Robert Magee	$75	00

Janitor, Washington County Court House.

Isaac T. Hopkins	$500	00

Janitor, Newport County Jail.

Archibald Alty	$500	00

Watchman, Newport County Jail.

Herman Rounds	$600	00

Watchman at Camp Ground, R. I. M.

Thomas C. Cole	$600	00

Care of Soldiers' and Sailors' Monument, Providence.

City of Providence..	$5 50
Richard Higgins..	44 50
	$50 00

Care of Stephen Hopkins' Monument.

North Burial Ground.......................................	$25 00

Care of Perry Monument, Newport.

Henry C. Stevens, Treasurer................................	$30 00

Care of Military Burial Ground, Dutch Island.

Nathan H. Baker...	$12 50

Rhode Island Historical Society.

Robert P. Brown, Treasurer................................	$1,500 00

Rhode Island Horticultural Society.

Charles W. Smith, Treasurer...............................	$1,000 00

Rhode Island Society, Prevention of Cruelty to Children.

Zephaniah Brown, Treasurer...............................	$2,500 00

Rhode Island Society, Prevention of Cruelty to Animals.

Albert Babcock, Treasurer.................................	$1,000 00

Newport Historical Society.

R. H. Tilley, Treasurer.....................................	$500 00

Newport Horticultural Society.

Andrew K. McMahon, Treasurer............................	$750 00

Newport County Agricultural Society.

E. R. Anthony, Treasurer..................................	$1,000 00

Washington County Agricultural Society.

Jesse V. B. Watson, Treasurer..............................	$1,000 00

Prisoners' Aid Association.

Mrs. Ervina O. S. Dow, Treasurer............................	$1,000 00

Rhode Island Poultry Association.

William H. Congdon, Treasurer..............................	$1,000 00

Providence Lying-in Hospital.

Edward L. Watson, Treasurer................................	$2,500 00

Saint Vincent de Paul Infant Asylum.

Dennis M. Lowney, Treasurer................................	$2,500 00

Care of District Rooms.

James Jeffrey...	$200 00
George S. Bennett...	104 00
Hiram Kimball..	52 00
Robert Magee...	48 00
	$404 00

B.

Pay and Mileage of the General Assembly.

Senate.

Henry F. Anthony, East Providence...........................	$310 24
Louis W. Arnold, Westerly..................................	287 64
James E. Bradford, Woonsocket.............................	346 08
Stephen H. Brown, Smithfield...............................	285 60
Norman L. Capwell, West Greenwich........................	364 00
William F. Caswell, Jamestown.............................	407 52
Christopher E. Champlin, New Shoreham.....................	466 40
James R. Chase, Middletown...............................	402 40
Thomas H. Connolly, Warren...............................	333 28
John S. Cole, Hopkinton...................................	417 76
Lyons Delany, Pawtucket..................................	312 80
Elisha Dyer, Providence...................................	302 56
C. Reginald Easton, Lincoln................................	323 04
John H. Edwards, Exeter..................................	384 48
Thomas H. Galvin, East Greenwich.........................	338 40
Herbert M. Gardiner, Barrington...........................	325 60
Horace F. Horton, Cranston................................	317 92
George R. Lawton, Tiverton................................	251 80
Andrew Luther, Burrillville................................	361 44

8

Thomas McKenna, Cumberland	333 28
Whiting Metcalf, Richmond	381 92
James A. Northup, Narragansett	394 72
Henry E. Nugent, Johnston	312 80
George W. Parrott, North Providence	315 36
James L. Phillips, Foster	366 56
Charles Potter, Glocester	361 44
John A. Remington, Central Falls	170 36
Benjamin F. Robinson, Jr., South Kingstown	381 92
Harry H. Shepard, Bristol	346 08
Henry A. Sisson, Coventry	364 00
Joseph E. Smith, North Kingstown	358 88
Walter R. Stiness, Warwick	273 28
Elbridge I. Stoddard, Portsmouth	374 24
Alphonso F. White, North Smithfield	351 20
Philip H. Wilbour, Little Compton	397 28
Eugene L. Young, Scituate	340 96
	$12,363 24

House of Representatives.

Joseph P. Burlingame, Warwick, Speaker	$615 36
Arthur W. Dennis, Providence, Deputy Speaker	307 68
Samuel W. K. Allen, East Greenwich	338 40
George J. Andrews, Coventry	340 96
Henry C. Anthony, Portsmouth	384 48
Latimer Willis Ballou, Woonsocket	346 08
Oscar A. Bennett, Woonsocket	346 08
Earl P. Blanchard, Foster	376 80
Zenas W. Bliss, Cranston	312 80
Walter A. Bowen, Warwick	333 28
William M. P. Bowen, Providence	305 12
John B. S. Brazeau, Pawtucket	312 80
Daniel W. Bullock, Pawtucket	310 24
Roswell B. Burchard, Little Compton	397 28
Robert S. Burlingame, Newport	412 64
James Y. Caldwell, Cumberland	330 72
Herbert L. Carpenter, North Smithfield	356 32
William P. Clarke, Newport	407 52
Everett A. Codlin, Westerly	417 76
Benjamin S. Cottrell, Jamestown	412 64
Albert B. Crafts, Westerly	357 64
George C. Cranston, North Kingstown	356 32
Elphege J. Daignault, Woonsocket	346 08
William T. Dodge, New Shoreham	453 60
J. Stephen Dolan, Central Falls	317 92
Giles W. Easterbrooks, Pawtucket	310 24
Jesse P. Eddy, Jr., Providence	305 12

George W. Estey, Providence	305	12
John J. Fitzgerald, Pawtucket	312	80
William I. Frost, Tiverton	376	80
Thomas J. Gaddes, Pawtucket	312	80
Charles C. Gauvin, Woonsocket	346	08
Euclide C. Gauvin, Burrillville	358	88
J. Fred Gibson, Providence	305	12
Henry C. Gorton, Providence	310	24
Thomas J. Gurry, Cumberland	320	48
James Harris, Smithfield	323	04
Horace N. Hassard, Newport	412	64
William H. Heimer, Pawtucket	312	80
Christopher L. Holden, Providence	312	80
George W. Hoxsie, Charlestown	384	48
Henry B. Kane, Narragansett	384	48
Joseph E. Lanphear, Richmond	381	92
M. Joseph E. Legris, Warwick	333	28
Louis L. Mailhot, Lincoln	335	84
Thomas E. Manney, Providence	305	12
Benjamin Martin, East Providence	312	80
John E. McKenna, North Providence	315	36
Philip A. Money, Exeter	369	12
James F. Murphy, Central Falls	315	36
Fred E. Newell, Central Falls	315	36
John North, Woonsocket	346	08
Henry A. Palmer, Cranston	312	80
Samuel L. Peck, Warren	328	16
George L. Pierce, Providence	305	12
Waldo M. Place, Providence	307	68
Amasa S. Potter, Scituate	330	72
Elmer J. Rathbun, West Greenwich	376	80
Herbert W. Rice, Providence	307	68
Stephen S. Rich, East Providence	307	68
John F. Richmond, Barrington	325	60
Albert Roberts, Providence	307	68
Andrew D. Ross, Pawtucket	312	80
William T. Stedman, South Kingstown	384	48
Lucius B. Steere, Glocester	335	84
John Veitch, Lincoln	325	60
George E. Vernon, Newport	335	60
John Walch, Johnston	315	36
Charles H. Ward, Middletown	412	64
William Fred Williams, Bristol	343	52
Clarence D. Wood, Hopkinton	407	52
J. Frank Woodmansee, Warwick	325	60
Joseph H. Hughes, Pawtucket	17	40
John G. Wilcox, Charlestown	412	64

$25,359 60

Recapitulation.

Senate..	$12,363 24
House of Representatives....................................	25,359 60
	$37,722 84

Officers of the General Assembly.

Osmond C. Goodell...	$370 00
Albert C. Johnson..	370 00
Thomas Dyer...	20 00
Andrew McKenzie..	20 00
Antonio Girardi..	20 00
Charles H. Brown..	20 00
Nathan Colvin...	20 00
Samuel E. Gardiner..	20 00
Edgar S. Thayer...	10 00
William P. Winslow..	10 00
Hugh F. McCusker...	10 00
Peter J. Healy...	10 00
Andre J. Blanchard..	10 00
Franklin B. Ham...	10 00
Herman Paster...	10 00
Daniel H. Horton..	10 00
	$940 00

Doorkeepers of the General Assembly.

Herbert G. Boyce..	$730 00
Robert B. Healey..	438 00
Arthur V. Warfield...	720 00
Joseph M. Provencher......................................	438 00
Charles C. Newhall..	402 00
Joseph O. Anthony...	438 00
	$3,166 00

Pages of the General Assembly.

Joseph F. Brennan...	$146 00
William E. Dodge..	142 00
William Harrison...	126 00
Clarence J. Lamb..	146 00
Robert E. Johnson...	148 00
Joseph H. McHugh...	148 00
Walter J. Lewis, Jr..	148 00
Abraham Bander...	148 00
Leon Lanoie	148 00
Edward O. Hustedt...	136 00

Herman Podrat	136	00
William W. Blodgett, Second	138	00
	$1,710	00

Stationery and Stamps for the General Assembly.

E. L. Freeman & Sons	$235	01
A. K. Goodwin, P. M.	60	00
Walter Price, P. M.	40	00
John W. Cass, P. M.	36	00
	$371	01

C.

Supreme and Superior Courts.

Jurors	$47,752	84
Officers	22,059	45
Witnesses	10,814	30
Incidentals	6,725	22
	$87,351	81

First Judicial District.

Officers	$1,390	05
Witnesses	570	50
	$1,960	55

Second Judicial District.

Officers	$648	25
Witnesses	117	10
	$765	35

Third Judicial District.

Officers	$644	95
Witnesses	226	80
	$871	75

Fourth Judicial District.

Officers	$526	35
Witnesses	358	90
	$885	25

Fifth Judicial District.

Officers	$1,055 25
Witnesses	422 30
	$1,477 55

Sixth Judicial District.

Officers	$2,868 75
Witnesses	3,318 20
	$6,186 95

Seventh Judicial District.

Officers	$919 35
Witnesses	245 50
	$1,164 85

Eighth Judicial District.

Officers	$700 50
Witnesses	436 60
	$1,137 10

Ninth Judicial District.

Officers	$396 10
Witnesses	138 80
	$534 90

Tenth Judicial District.

Officers	$1,338 90
Witnesses	357 80
	$1,696 70

Eleventh Judicial District.

Officers	$1,401 80
Witnesses	267 20
	$1,669 00

Twelfth Judicial District.

Officers	$1,074 40
Witnesses	289 80
	$1,364 20

Wardens' Court, New Shoreham.

Officers..	$26 50
Witnesses..	10 00
	$36 50
Officers in Criminal Cases..................................	$8,690 35

D.

Orders of the Governor, Civil Account........................	$2,534 67
Orders of the Governor, Criminal Account....................	524 29
	$3,058 96

E.

State Printing...	$39,999 62
State Binding...	8,994 00
Advertising and Publishing Public Laws......................	5,650 62

F.

State Institutions in Cranston, support of.....................	$342,387 19
State Home and School, support of..........................	21,590 56
State Board of Agriculture..................................	19,046 66
Rhode Island College of Agriculture and Mechanics Arts.........	15,000 00

G.

State Normal School.......................................	$63,999 76
Mileage, State Normal School...............................	4,000 00
Teachers' Institutes.......................................	110 75
Teachers' Examinations....................................	2,264 48
Graded and High Schools...................................	17,630 00
Evening Schools...	4,853 40
Lectures and Addresses, Public Schools......................	164 01
School Apparatus..	3,575 63
Public Libraries...	7,486 75
Rhode Island School of Design..............................	5,951 75
Rhode Island Institute for the Deaf.........................	19,963 98
Education of Blind and Imbecile.............................	15,997 51
Supervision of Public Schools...............................	10,750 00

Public Schools.

July 15.	Barrington.......................................	$1,000 00
	Bristol...	1,500 00
	Burrillville.....................................	1,500 00

July 15.	Central Falls	1,500 00
	Charlestown	700 00
	Coventry	1,500 00
	Cranston	1,500 00
	Cumberland	1,500 00
	East Greenwich	1,400 00
	East Providence	1,500 00
	Exeter	1,100 00
	Foster	1,400 00
	Glocester	1,300 00
	Hopkinton	1,500 00
	Jamestown	500 00
	Johnston	1,500 00
	Lincoln	1,500 00
	Little Compton	900 00
	Middletown	500 00
	Narragansett	700 00
	Newport	1,500 00
	New Shoreham	600 00
	North Kingstown	1,500 00
	North Providence	1,300 00
	North Smithfield	1,400 00
	Pawtucket	1,500 00
	Portsmouth	900 00
	Providence	1,500 00
	Richmond	1,100 00
	Scituate	1,500 00
	Smithfield	1,200 00
	South Kingstown	1,500 00
	Tiverton	1,500 00
	Warren	1,498 50
	Warwick	1,500 00
	Westerly	1,500 00
	West Greenwich	1,200 00
	Woonsocket	1,500 00
		$48,698 50
Dec. 15.	Barrington	$280 33
	Bristol	1,136 29
	Burrillville	1,108 63
	Central Falls	2,820 54
	Charlestown	122 60
	Coventry	981 55
	Cranston	2,090 18
	Cumberland	1,577 35
	East Greenwich	500 87
	East Providence	2,348 09

Dec. 15.	Exeter	91 20
	Foster	150 26
	Glocester	213 80
	Hopkinton	370 04
	Jamestown	140 54
	Johnston	885 11
	Lincoln	1,524 27
	Little Compton	153 25
	Middletown	186 14
	Narragansett	177 92
	Newport	3,119 57
	New Shoreham	171 94
	North Kingstown	648 13
	North Providence	554 69
	North Smithfield	411 16
	Pawtucket	6,988 19
	Portsmouth	287 06
	Providence	28,117 97
	Richmond	162 22
	Scituate	461 24
	Smithfield	294 54
	South Kingstown	771 48
	Tiverton	564 41
	Warren	784 94
	Warwick	4,301 46
	Westerly	1,144 51
	West Greenwich	79 99
	Woonsocket	5,577 54

$71,300 00

Recapitulation.

Apportionment due July 15, 1905	$48,698 50
Apportionment due December 15, 1905	71,300 00
Fines Credited to Permanent School Fund	1 50

$120,000 00

H.

Special Appropriations.

Furnishing Old State House for Sixth District Court	$160 00
Furniture, etc., State Sealer	78 00
Care and Maintenance, New State House	38,921 74
Purchase of Publications, Soldiers' and Sailors' Historical Society	61 20
Printing and Binding Volume 6, R. I. Reports	1,339 50
Inland Fisheries	7,682 23
Transfer of Battle Flags	555 62

9

Purchase of Markers for Soldiers' and Sailors' Graves.............	206 20
Repairs and Improvements, State Building, Charlestown..........	300 00
Construction and Furnishing State Hospital for Insane..........	4,271 45
Colonial and Revolutionary War Records......................	431 35
Land Titles, Kent and Washington Counties...................	11 20
Protection, Devil's Breach, Charlestown......................	336 57
Bounty for Foxes..	194 00
Bounty for Wild Crows and Hawks............................	415 25
State Sanatorium...	48,126 78
State Sanatorium for Consumptives..........................	25,500 02
Construction, R. I. Stone Bridge.............................	53,969 96
Providence Armory..	1,000 00
Grading and Improving Land, Indian Burial Ground Hill........	39 15
Newspaper Records of Early Deaths in Rhode Island............	2,000 00
Repairing State Armory, East Greenwich......................	128 32
State Representation at Expositions and Celebrations...........	2,494 96
Repairing Heating Apparatus, Bristol Armory..................	930 00
Supreme Court Commission...................................	2,344 77
Temporary Quarters and Court Facilities, Supreme and Superior Courts, Providence County.............................	72,162 34
Louisiana Purchase Exposition...............................	2,703 92
Control and Prevention of Tuberculosis.......................	1,496 16
Instruction of the Adult Blind...............................	1,912 49
Causes and Prevention of Diphtheria..........................	1,758 74
Repairs and Furnishings, Providence County Court House........	33 38
Breachway at Block Island...................................	952 00
Construction of an Inner Harbor, Block Island.................	128 81
Agricultural Demonstrations.................................	3,680 06
Repairs and Improvements at R. I. College of Agriculture..........	2,155 01
Shipping Interests of the State in Providence Harbor.............	684 37
Construction and Improvements, State Highways...............	100,339 54
Expense of Opening Breachway at South Kingstown.............	123 12
Proceeds of Camp Ground, R. I. M...........................	383 19
Expenses of Metropolitan Park Commission....................	957 27
Reclaiming Burial Place of Governor Benedict Arnold...........	15 00
Repairing State Arsenal, Providence..........................	1,225 30
Repairing Newport County Jail...............................	194 00
Industrial Education at Sockanosset School....................	489 83
Rifle Practice, State Militia.................................	4,999 83
Expenses of State Sealer.....................................	27 86
Repairs and Alterations, State Rifle Range....................	1,100 00
State Census...	18,939 37
Compensation of Supreme Court Commission....................	17,500 00
Expenses, Shell Fish Commissioners, Investigating pollution of Providence River..	1,200 94
U. S. Volunteer Life Saving Corps............................	170 34
Purchase of Library of the Late G. F. Keene, M. D..............	1,200 00
Deficiency Account, R. I. College of Agriculture................	5,000 00

Repairing Newport County Court House........................ 1,032 56
Expenses, J. S. Committee on Ballot Reform.................... 1,095 31
Interest on money borrowed.................................. 15,508 50

$450,667 51

I.

Miscellaneous Accounts.

Clerk hire and incidentals, Law Library........................ $499 18
Accounts allowed by the General Assembly..................... 4,524 88
Traveling expenses of Justices of the Supreme Court............ 864 61
Traveling expenses of Attorney-General and Assistant........... 60 49
Traveling expenses of Stenographic Clerks...................... 645 56
Court Stenographers, Supreme and Superior Courts.............. 2,559 77
Investment of Permanent School Fund........................ 4,516 98
State Board of Health...................................... 5,998 81
State Board of Public Roads................................. 4,999 31
State Library.. 397 61
Law Library... 2,297 29
Law Library, Supreme Court................................ 1,702 18
Indigent Insane.. 10,000 00
Providence County Court House............................. 4,498 71
Old State House... 479 50
Woonsocket Court House.................................... 496 47
Public Buildings, Newport County............................ 1,298 57
Public Buildings, Washington County......................... 496 56
Public Buildings, Kent County............................... 429 49
Public Buildings, Bristol County............................. 313 02
Militia and Military Affairs................................. 37,499 84
Armory Rents, R. I. Militia................................. 7,141 03
Heating and Lighting Armories.............................. 3,300 00
Storage and Care of Equipments, R. I. M..................... 700 00
Medical Examiners and Coroners............................. 4,999 74
Jails and Jailers.................... .... 1,470 02
Fuel and Gas.. 10,621 77
Rents... 1,658 25
Fines in Certain Cases..................................... 2,028 00
Soldiers' Home Fund....................................... 37,482 51
Soldiers' Relief Fund...................................... 9,843 00
Commissioners of Sinking Fund.............................. 41,000 00
Interests on Bonds, State House Construction Loan............. 87,000 00
Interest on Land Grant Fund, 1862.......................... 534 22
Commercial Fertilizers..................................... 2,200 61
Commercial Feeding Stuffs.................................. 1,194 59
Expenses Enforcing Laws Relating to Shell Fisheries........... 1,180 00
Expenses of Factory Inspectors.............................. 556 34
Expenses of Commissioners of Birds.......................... 264 36
Expenses of Commissioner of Industrial Statistics.............. 2,999 26

Expenses of State Record Commissioner...............................	594	39
Expenses of State Board Soldiers' Relief.............................	1,093	22
Expenses of Commissioner of Dams and Reservoirs................	160	00
Expenses of Commissioners on Uniformity of Legislation.........	200	00
Expenses of Attorney-General's Department.....................	863	76
Expenses of Railroad Commissioner.............................	633	04
Expenses of State Returning Board.............................	1,013	44
Clerk Hire and Incidentals, State Librarian.....................	500	00
Miscellaneous Expenses.......................................	12,000	00

STATE INDEBTEDNESS.

Floating Debt.

Notes, Rhode Island Hospital Trust Company...................	$100,000	00
Notes, Industrial Trust Company..............................	100,000	00
Note, Commissioners of Sinking Fund.........................	45,000	00
	$245,000	00

Bonded Debt.

400 Three and one-half per cent. bonds, for, Construction of State House, due January, 1914...............................	$400,000	00
400 Three and one-half per cent. bonds, for construction of State House, due January, 1924.................................	400,000	00
400 Three and one-half per cent. bonds, for construction of State House, due January, 1934.................................	400,000	00
800 Three per cent. bonds, for construction of State House, due July, 1938..	800,000	00
700 Three per cent. bonds, for construction of State House, due May, 1941...	700,000	00
	$2,700,000	00
Cash and Securities in Sinking Fund, for Liquidation of State House Bonds..	359,559	21
	$2,340,440	79

Recapitulation.

Floating Debt...	$245,000	00
Bonded Debt...	2,700,000	00
	$2,945,000	00
Amount of interest paid on State House bonds during the year ending December 31, 1905...............................	$87,000	00

At the close of the year ending December 31, 1905, there were no coupons due and unpaid.

Respectfully submitted,

WALTER A. READ,

General Treasurer.

APPENDIX.

List of Bonds, Coupons, and Certificates of Indebtedness Redeemed and Destroyed February 18, 1905, in Accordance with the Provisions of Section 3, Chapter 32, of the General Laws, with the Number, Date of Issue, and the Denomination of Each Bond, Coupon, and Certificate.

July, 1863.

Coupon bonds numbers 004, 015, 016, 017, 018, 019, 020, 022, 025, 030, 041, 042, 067, 211, 212, 324, 327, 587, 588, 589, 590, 591, 853, 887, 888, for $1,000 each............................ $25,000 00

August, 1864.

Coupon bonds numbers 010, 011, 139, 363, 372, 505, 506, 507, 574, 575, 576, 577, 578, 701, 758, for $1,000 each................ $15,000 00

November 8, 1867.

Registered certificate number 58, for $5,000; 59, for $5,000; 60, for $5,000; 61, for $5,000; 62, for $5,000; 63, for $5,000; 64, for $5,000; 65, for $5,000; 66, for $5,000; 67, for $5,000; amounting to... $50,000 00

May 6, 1870.

Registered certificate number 83, for........................... $4,000 00

June 9, 1871.

Registered certificate number 126, for.......................... $10,000 00

January 9, 1873.

Registered certificate number 154, for.......................... $1,000 00

February 21, 1873.

Registered certificate number 157, for $15,000; 159, for $10,000; amounting to... $25,000 00

April 12, 1873.

Registered certificate number 164, for......................... $2,000 00

March 26, 1874.

Registered certificate number 176, for $5,000; 177, for $5,000;
 amounting to.. $10,000 00

October 12, 1874.

Registered certificate number 189, for $10,000; 190, for $10,000;
 191, for $10,000; 192, for $10,000; 193, for $10,000; amount-
 ing to.. $50,000 00

October 23, 1875.

Registered certificate number 203, for $10,000; 204, for $10,000;
 205, for $10,000; 206, for $10,000; 207, for $10,000; amount-
 ing to.....:.. $50,000 00

May 7, 1877.

Registered certificate number 231, for $4,000 00................. $4,000 00

April 24, 1878.

Registered certificate number 237, for $5,000; 238, for $5,000;
 amounting to.. $10,000 00

November 19, 1878.

Registered certificate number 268, for $5,000; 269, for $5,000; 270,
 for $5,000; 271, for $5,000; 272, for $5,000; 273, for $5,000;
 274, for $5,000; 275, for $5,000; 276, for $5,000; 277, for
 $5,000; 278, for $5,000; 279, for $5,000; 280, for $5,000; 281,
 for $5,000; 282, for $5,000; 283, for $5,000; 284, for $5,000;
 285, for $5,000; 286, for $5,000; 287, for $5,000; amounting to $100,000 00

February 21, 1882.

Registered certificate number 313, for......................... $4,000 00

October 20, 1883.

Registered certificate number 319, for $10,000; 320, for $10,000;
 321, for $5,000; 322, for $1,000; amounting to.............. $26,000 00

March 5, 1884.

Registered certificate number 327, for $1,000; 331, for $1,000;
 332, for $1,000; 334, for $1,000; amounting to............. $4,000 00

March 31, 1884.

Registered certificate number 337, for......................... $50,000 00

March 6, 1885.

Registered certificate number 344, for......................... $3,000 00

February 18, 1887.

Registered certificate number 347, for......................... $1,000 00

March 3, 1887.

Registered certificate number 348, for......................... $50,000 00

January 9, 1888.

Registered certificate number 354, for......................... $1,000 00

September 24, 1888.

Registered certificate number 356, for $10,000; 357, for $15,000;
amounting to.. $25,000 00

October 18, 1888.

Registered certificate number 358, for $4,000; 359, for $13,000;
amounting to.. $17,000 00

October 26, 1888.

Registered certificate number 361, for......................... $4,000 00

January 1, 1889.

Registered certificate number 362, for $1,000; 363, for $1,000; 364,
for $3,000; 365, for $1,000; 366, for $1,000; 367, for $1,000;
368, for $1,000; 369, for $1,000; 370, for $3,000; 371, for
$1,000; 372, for $5,000; amounting to..................... $19,000 00

February 13, 1889.

Registered certificate number 373, for......................... $5,000 00

October 31, 1889.

Registered certificate number 377, for......................... $1,000 00

August 2, 1890.

Registered certificate number 380, for......................... $1,000 00

April 29, 1891.

Registered certificate number 382, for $10,000; 383, for $10,000; 384, for $5,000; 385, for $5,000; 386, for $10,000; 387, for $10,000; amounting to.................................. $50,000 00

October 14, 1874.

Registered certificate number 196, for $1,000; 197, for $5,000; 198, for $5,000; 199, for $5,000; amounting to.................. $16,000 00

STATE HOUSE CONSTRUCTION LOAN BONDS.

January 1, 1894.

Registered bonds numbers 13, 14, 15, 16, 17, 18, 19, 20, 21, 22, 23, 24, 25, 26, 27, 28, 29, 30, 31, 32, 33, 34, 35, 36, 37, 38, 39, 40, 41, 42, 90, 91, 92, 93, 94, 95, 96, 97, 98, 99, 100, 101, 102, 103, 104, 105, 106, 107, 108, 109, 226, 227, 228, 229, 230, 231, 232, 233, 234, 235 236, 237, 238, 239, 240, 241, 242, 243, 244, 245, 246, 247, 248, 249, 250, 251, 252, 253, 254, 255, for $1,000 each, amounting to... $80,000 00
Coupon bonds numbers 1, 2, 3, 4, 5, 6, 7, 8, 9, 10, 11, 12, 43, 44, 45, 46, 47, 48, 49, 50, 51, 52, 53, 54, 55, 56, 57, 58, 59, 60, 61, 62, 63, 64, 65, 66, 67, 68, 69, 70, 71, 72, 73, 74, 75, 76, 77, 78, 79, 80, 81, 82, 83, 84, 85, 86, 87, 88, 89, 110, 111, 112, 113, 114, 115, 116, 117, 118, 119, 120, 121, 122, 123, 124, 125, 126, 127, 128, 129, 130, 131, 132, 133, 134, 135, 136, 137, 138, 139, 140, 141, 142, 143, 144, 145, 146, 147, 148, 149, 150, 151, 152, 153, 154, 155, 156, 157, 158, 159, 160, 161, 162, 163, 164, 165, 166, 167, 168, .169, 170, 171, 172, 173, 174, 175, 176, 177, 178, 179, 180, 181, 182, 183, 184, 185, 186, 187, 188, 189, 190, 191, 192, 193, 194, 195, 196, 197, 198, 199, 200, 201, 202, 203, 204, 205, 206, 207, 208, 209, 210, 211, 212, 213, 214, 215, 216, 217, 218, 219, 220, 221, 222, 223, 224, 225, 256, 257, 258, 259, 260, 261, 262, 263, 264, 265, 266, 267, 268, 269, 270, 271, 272, 273, 274, 275, 276, 277, 278, 279, 280, 281, 282, 283, 284, 285, 286, 287, 288, 289, 290, 291, 292, 293, 294, 295, 296, 297, 298, 299, 300, for $1,000 each, amounting to..................................... $220,000 00

We hereby certify that the bonds and certificates of indebtedness of the numbers, dates of issue, and denominations hereinbefore set forth, with their coupons, which have become the property of the State, not held by the Commissioners of Sinking Fund, have been this day, in our presence, destroyed by burning by the General Treasurer.

> CHARLES P. BENNETT, *Secretary of State.*
> CHARLES C. GRAY, *State Auditor.*
Attest: WILLIAM B. GREENOUGH, *Attorney-General.*
> WALTER A. READ, *General Treasurer.*

COMMISSIONERS OF SINKING FUND.

Established by Chapter 32, General Laws.

STATE HOUSE CONSTRUCTION.

Cash and securities reported December 31, 1904................		$317,135 83
General Treasurer's check...................................		41,000 00
Interest on investments to December 31, 1905................		11,629 98
		$369,765 81
Paid interest, note, Industrial Trust Company........	$206 60	
Cancelled note, Industrial Trust Company...........	10,000 00	
Bonds, notes and cash..........................	359,559 21	$369,765 81

The Fund is invested as follows:

Notes, Town of New Shoreham...............................	$44,000 00
18 Town of Cumberland 4 per cent. bonds.....................	18,000 00
12 District of Narragansett 4 per cent. bonds..................	12,000 00
50 Town of Cranston 4 per cent. bonds.......................	57,905 56
25 Town of Jamestown 4 per cent. bonds.....................	27,585 83
30 Town of Jamestown 3½ per cent. bonds.....................	31,352 92
32 Town of Bristol 3½ per cent. bonds........................	33,880 53
53 City of Woonsocket Water Works Improvement 4 per cent. bonds.	58,382 66
20 City of Woonsocket 4 per cent. sewer bonds................	22,119 44
5 Town of East Providence Fire District 4½ per cent. bonds......	5,811 88
Note, State of Rhode Island.................................	45,000 00
Cash on call, R. I. Hospital Trust Company....................	2,380 97
Cash on call, Industrial Trust Company.......................	1,139 42
	$359,559 21

OFFICE OF SINKING FUND COMMISSION,

PROVIDENCE, R. I., December 26, 1905.

The undersigned hereby certify they have personally examined the securities and investments constituting the State House Construction Sinking Fund in the custody of the General Treasurer, and find them to agree with the statement set forth in his annual report.

GEORGE H. UTTER,
ZENAS W. BLISS,
ELBRIDGE I. STODDARD,
EBEN N. LITTLEFIELD,
CHARLES C. GRAY,

Commissioners.

TOURO JEWISH SYNAGOGUE FUND.

Balance January 1, 1905......................................		$48,175 87
Dividend, Blackstone Canal National Bank............	$250 00	
Dividend, Savings Bank of Newport.................	1,254 11	
Dividend, Newport National Bank....................	113 40	
Dividend, Manufacturers Trust Company.............	180 00	
Dividend, Merchants National Bank.................	96 00	
Dividend, United National Bank....................	40 00	
Interest, Industrial Trust Company.................	278 86	
Interest, R. I. Hospital Trust Company..............	167 99	
Interest, call account, R. I. Hospital Trust Company...	15 32	
Interest, call account, Industrial Trust Company......	30 18	2,425 86
Dividend Number 2, Weybosset National Bank, in liquidation....................................	500 00	
Dividend Number 3, Weybosset National Bank, in liquidation.......................................	100 00	600 00
		$51,201 73
Deposit, Savings Bank of Newport................... $35,546 93		
Deposit, Industrial Trust Company, participation account.......................................	7,557 99	
Deposit, R. I. Hospital Trust Company, participation account.......................................	4,926 51	
Deposit, R. I. Hospital Trust Company, call account....	1,349 86	
Deposit, Industrial Trust Company, call account.......	1,720 44	
Paid Agent to June 30, 1905........................	100 00	$51,201 73

List of Stocks Held by the Touro Jewish Synagogue Fund.

21 shares Newport National Bank.
200 shares Blackstone Canal National Bank.
30 shares Manufacturers Trust Company.
32 shares Merchants National Bank.
5 shares United National Bank.
20 shares Weybosset National Bank in liquidation.
18 shares Lime Rock National Bank in liquidation.

LAND GRANT FUND, 1862.

Act of Congress, July 2, 1862.

Amount received from Brown University......................		$50,000 00
Interest, participation account, Industrial Trust Company..	$1,965 78	
General Treasurer's check.........................	534 22	2,500 00
		$52,500 00

Paid treasurer, R. I. College of Agriculture and Mechanic Arts......	$2,500 00
Deposit, Industrial Trust Company............................	50,000 00

$52,500 00

THE PERMANENT SCHOOL FUND.

Established, October Session, 1836.

The following is a list of investments of the Fund:

115 Town of Lincoln 4 per cent. gold bonds....................	$129,547 50
20 Town of Warren 4 per cent. gold bonds....................	22,162 83
16 Town of Johnston 4 per cent. gold bonds..................	17,282 85
25 Town of East Providence 4 per cent. gold bonds.............	26,247 17
28 Town of Bristol 3½ per cent. gold bonds..................	29,645 47
406 shares National Bank of Commerce......................	22,585 24
1 Town of Cranston 4 per cent. gold bond...................	1,160 44
3 City of Woonsocket 4 per cent. gold bonds.................	3,347 00
Cash available for investment................................	5,434 36

$257,412 86

Fines deducted from appropriation for Public Schools in accordance with Chapter 1114 of the Public Laws:

Town of Warren...	1 50

$257,414 36

ANDERSONVILLE MONUMENT FUND.

Resolution of General Assembly, passed December, 1902.

Fund for Perpetual Care of Monument and Lot on Prison Property, Andersonville, Georgia..........	$500 00	
Interest, Industrial Trust Company.................	20 20	
		$520 20
Paid Chairman, Board of Managers, Woman's Relief Corps, Andersonville, Georgia...................	$20 20	
Deposit, Industrial Trust Company.................	500 00	
		$520 20

HATCH FUND.

Act of Congress, August 30, 1890.

United States Treasury check................................	$25,000 00
Paid treasurer, R. I. College of Agriculture and Mechanic Arts......	$25,000 00

FIREMEN'S RELIEF FUND.

Established by Chapter 1161, Public Laws.

Appropriation..	$2,500 00
Paid Frederic W. Cady, treasurer..............................	$2,500 00

LIST OF UNEXPENDED BALANCES OF SPECIAL APPROPRIATIONS.

Care and maintenance of new State House	$12,947 88
Inland Fisheries...	1,678 99
Construction and Furnishing State Hospital for Insane...........	968 91
Land titles, Kent and Washington Connty......................	238 80
Protection of Devil's Breach at Charlestown Pond..............	157 82
Construction of R. I. Stone Bridge............................	114,605 64
Providence Armory...	2,989 69
State Representation at Expositions and Celebrations...........	2,505 04
Instruction of Adult Blind....................................	1,831 30
Causes and Prevention of Diphtheria..........................	1,290 28
Agricultural Demonstrations.....................	1,610 20
Repairs and improvements at R. I. College of Agriculture........	619 78
Shipping interests of State in Providence Harbor.................	4,315 63
Construction and improvement of State roads..................	35,874 54
Expense opening breachway at South Kingstown................	4,473 83
Reclaiming burial place of Governor Benedict Arnold............	852 81
Repairing State Arsenal, Providence...........................	1,924 70
Industrial education at Sockanosset School.....................	1,361 71
State census...	1,060 63
Expense of Shell Fish Commissioners investigating Providence river..	799 06
Repairing Newport County Court House........................	774 61
R. I. College of Agriculture building account...................	20,000 00
John Waterman Memorial......................................	10,000 00
Treatment of Feeble-Minded Children..........................	500 00
Relocating monuments, City of Providence.....................	15,000 00
Purchase of Land, etc., State Farm............................	258 13
Soldiers' Home Fund...	3,802 93
Miscellaneous...	867 74
	$243,310 65

STATE VALUATION.

As established by Chapter 1246 of the Public Laws, passed May 11, 1905. Rate of tax: eighteen cents on each one hundred dollars, payable one-half, June 15, and one-half, December 15, in each year.

	Valuation.	Tax.
Providence...............................	$222,391,940 00	$400,305 50
North Providence.........................	1,884,900 00	3,392 82
East Providence..........................	9,918,225 00	17,852 80

	Valuation.	Tax.
Pawtucket	38,629,480 00	69,533 06
Lincoln	4,831,428 00	8,696 58
Central Falls	8,831,340 00	15,896 42
Smithfield	1,733,642 00	3,120 56
North Smithfield	2,052,095 00	3,693 78
Woonsocket	17,283,850 00	31,110 94
Cumberland	8,623,124 00	15,521 62
Burrillville	4,048,700 00	7,287 66
Glocester	1,081,875 00	1,947 38
Foster	509,750 00	917 56
Scituate	2,443,000 00	4,397 40
Johnston	2,548,920 00	4,588 06
Cranston	14,527,217 00	26,149 00
Newport	56,626,700 00	101,928 06
Middletown	3,097,975 00	5,576 36
Portsmouth	3,118,375 00	5,613 08
Tiverton	3,099,847 00	5,579 72
Little Compton	1,463,070 00	2,633 52
Jamestown	2,621,630 00	4,718 94
New Shoreham	908,800 00	1,635 84
Warren	4,595,900 00	8,272 62
Bristol	5,888,000 00	10,598 40
Barrington	2,777,875 00	·5,000 18
North Kingstown	4,409,920 00	7,937 86
South Kingstown	5,298,330 00	9,537 00
Narragansett	3,701,500 00	6,662 70
Charlestown	844,300 00	1,519 74
Westerly	7,312,600 00	13,162 68
Hopkinton	1,729,450 00	3,113 02
Richmond	1,182,235 00	2,128 02
Exeter	509,195 00	916 56
Warwick	20,093,160 00	36,167 68
Coventry	4,029,400 00	7,252 92
East Greenwich	2,377,220 00	4,279 00
West Greenwich	352,690 00	634 84
	$477,377,658 00	$859,279 88

TRUST COMPANIES.

State, municipal, and town bonds and securities have been deposited with the General Treasurer as a guarantee fund, by trust companies acting as executors, administrators, and trustees, in accordance with the provisions of their acts of incorporation, as enumerated below:

Industrial Trust Company	$618,388 64
Rhode Island Hospital Trust Company	200,000 00

Manufacturers Trust Company	100,000	00
Slater Trust Company	100,000	00
Newport Trust Company	60,000	00
Union Trust Company	50,000	00
Washington Trust Company	40,000	00
Phenix Trust Company	22,000	00
Title Guarantee Company of Rhode Island	20,000	00
Producers Trust Company	1,000	00

SOURCES AND AUTHORITY OF STATE REVENUE.

STATE TAX.

CHAPTER 29, SECTION 1.—A tax of eighteen cents on each one hundred dollars of the ratable property of the several towns as herein set forth shall be annually assessed, collected, and paid by the several towns to the General Treasurer, one-half thereof on or before the fifteenth day of June, and one-half thereof on or before the fifteenth day of December in each year.

Amount, 1905.......................... $798,590 10.

INSTITUTIONS FOR SAVINGS.

CHAPTER 29. SECTIONS 3 AND 4.—Every institution for savings shall annually pay to the General Treasurer forty cents on each one hundred dollars deposited therewith, and on each one hundred dollars of reserve profits, said sums to be ascertained from the returns required to be made to the State Auditor, and to be paid on or before the first Monday in August.

Trust companies the same.

Amount, 1905................................ $435,299 49

STATE INSURANCE COMPANIES.

CHAPTER 29, SECTION 5.—Every insurance company incorporated and doing business in this State shall annually, on the first Monday in April, pay to the General Treasurer two per centum of the gross premiums and assessments received on property insured by said company during the year ending on the thirty-first day of December preceding, on property insured by said company within this State and on property insured in any other State on which such company has not paid and is not liable to pay a tax to such other State.

Amount, 1905............................. $92,037 74

FOREIGN INSURANCE AND SURETY COMPANIES.

CHAPTER 29, SECTION 6.—Every agent of an insurance company, co-operative or otherwise, and every agent of a surety company not incorporated by the

State, doing business or residing therein shall, during the month of January in every year, make returns to the General Treasurer of the amount insured or procured to be insured by him, and by his sub-agents in this State, during the year preceding, and of the amount of premiums received, and assessments collected, during the said period; and shall at the same time pay to the General Treasurer a tax of two per centum on the amount of such premiums and assessments.

Amount, 1905... $127,004 63

FOREIGN BUILDING–LOAN ASSOCIATIONS.

CHAPTER 189, SECTION 6.—Every building-loan association admitted to do business under the provisions of this chapter shall before the first day of February in each year pay a tax to the General Treasurer of this State equal to one-fourth of one per centum on the amount of the capital actually paid in to December thirty-first of the preceding year, from residents of this State, less the amount of all certificates withdrawn, and less, also, the amount of its outstanding loans secured by its shares on bond and mortgage and on real estate within this State and secured by its shares pledged by residents of this State; and said building-loan association and its shares shall be exempt from payment of any other tax whatsoever, except it shall be assessed for and pay a tax on all real estate acquired in this State in the course of its business.

Amount, 1905....................................None.

JAILERS.

CHAPTER 35, SECTION 25.—Sheriffs, deputy sheriffs, jailers, and other persons, except clerks of courts and justices of district courts, receiving fines, penalties, and forfeitures accruing or belonging to the State, or costs due or payable into the State treasury, shall, as often as twice a year, account with the auditor for the same.

Amount, 1905...............................$6,277 57

SUPREME COURT.

CHAPTER 34, SECTION 15.—Each of the clerks of either division of the supreme court, if and so far as the provisions of this section shall be applicable, shall respectively, within twenty days after the close of any session thereof, in counties other than the county of Providence, and within twenty days after the fifteenth day of February, May, August, and November in the county of Providence, render a true and particular account to the State Auditor of all fines, penalties, and forfeitures imposed or declared forfeit, and of all recognizance defaulted, and of all judgments rendered in favor of the State or of any officer for the benefit of the State, at such session, or during such preceding quarter, as the case may be; also copies of all bills of costs taxed and actually paid, in whole or in part, in criminal prosecutions, or in any other case in which the State or the General

Treasurer may be a party; also copies of all allowances for extraordinary and incidental services and expenses, and also of all moneys belonging to the State received by him from any source whatever; which account shall be accompanied by a certificate from one of the justices of the respective division of said court, verifying the same, and specifying therein the number of cases tried or open to the jury and the amount of fines imposed for non-attendance of jurors.

Amount, 1905................................. $13,175 56

DISTRICT COURTS.

Same section. And clerks of district courts shall as often as once in three months render a like account to the State Auditor.

Amount, 1905.............................. $27,793 55

TELEGRAPH AND TELEPHONE COMPANIES.

CHAPTER 29, SECTION 12.—Every telegraph company and every telephone company doing business within this State shall annually, on the first Monday in July, make return to the State Auditor, subscribed and sworn to by its treasurer or agent within this State, setting forth all the gross receipts of such company derived from its business transacted within this State from whatever source the same may come, whether from the transmission of messages, the use of machines or otherwise, and shall thereafter annually, on or before the first day of August next succeeding the making of such return, pay to the General Treasurer a tax of one per centum on such gross receipts for the use of the State, which sum shall be in lieu of all other taxes upon its lines and personal estate used exclusively in telegraphic and telephone business within this State.

Amount, 1905.............................. $8,423 34

EXPRESS COMPANIES.

CHAPTER 29, SECTION 13.—Every express company doing business within this State shall annually, on the first Monday in July, make return to the State Auditor, subscribed and sworn to by its principal officer or agent within this State, setting forth all the gross receipts of such company derived from its business transacted within the State from whatever source it may come, and shall thereafter annually, on or before the first day of August next succeeding the making of such return, pay to the General Treasurer a tax of one per centum on such gross receipts for the use of the State, which sum shall be in lieu of all other taxes upon its personal estate used exclusively in the express business.

Amount, 1905................................. $531 14

CHARTERS, CORPORATIONS.

CHAPTER 29, SECTION 16.—No corporation other than a corporation for religious, literary, or charitable purposes, or a military or fire company, shall be

11

organized under a charter granted by special act of the General Assembly, until the petitioners for the same shall pay into the general treasury for the use of the State one hundred dollars, and in addition one-tenth of one per centum upon any amount of capital stock exceeding one hundred thousand dollars authorized by such charter; and every corporation which shall increase its capital stock shall pay into the general treasury, for the use of the State, one-tenth of one per centum upon such increase; and the Secretary of State shall not issue a certified copy of any act creating such corporation, or providing for such increase of capital stock, until he shall receive the certificate of the General Treasurer to the effect that the sum so required has been paid.

Amount, 1905............................... $38,217 50

TOWN COUNCILS, LICENSES.

CHAPTER 102, SECTION 2.— . . . . and he shall also pay for such licenses to the town or city treasurer the sum hereinafter named, three-fourths thereof for the use of such town or city, and one-fourth to be paid over by the town or city treasurer to the General Treasurer for the use of the State.

Also SECTION 64.—The treasurer of every town and city shall, on the tenth day of July and January in each year, make returns to the General Treasurer of all moneys coming to his hands belonging to the State, received under the provisions of this chapter, which return shall embrace the names of the persons from whom received and the amount received from each person.

Also one-half of sums received from licenses for shows, billiard, pool, and bagatelle tables, etc.

Amount, 1905............................... $128,995 76

PEDDLERS' LICENSES.

CHAPTER 162, SECTION 6.—The General Treasurer may grant and issue, to any person he may deem suitable, a license for the whole State or for any one of the counties, for offering for sale and for selling, as a hawker and peddler, watches, jewelry, gold or silverware, or articles manufactured of German silver, upon the payment to the General Treasurer for the use of the State the following sums: two hundred dollars for a license as aforesaid for the State, one hundred dollars for the county of Providence, and fifty dollars for each of the other counties; and may grant and issue a license for offering for sale and for selling, as a hawker and peddler, any other goods, wares, and merchandise whatsoever, except as hereinafter provided, for the State or any of the counties, upon the payment to the General Treasurer for the use of the State of the following sums: sixty dollars for a license for the State for one year from the date of the license, fifteen dollars for the State for three months from the date of the license, thirty dollars for the county of Providence for one year from the date of the license, ten dollars for the county of Providence for three months from the date of the license, fifteen dollars for each of the counties for one year from the date of the license, fifteen dollars for the city of Providence for one year from the date of the license, and five dollars for the city of Providence for three months from the date of the license; and a license for the whole State only as a hawker and peddler for offering for sale and for selling any article which, by reason of the protection afforded by the patent of the United States or otherwise, does not come into competition with the general sale thereof in the towns of the State, upon the payment of fifty dollars, for the use of the State.

Amount, 1905................................. $1,905 00

DUTY ON AUCTION PROPERTY.

CHAPTER 159, SECTION 12.—The duty upon all property sold by auction in the State and which is liable to duty, shall be one-tenth of one per centum, and shall enure one-eighth part thereof to the use of the town in which such sales shall be made, and the remainder thereof to the use of the State.

Amount, 1905................................. $1,628 79

PERMANENT SCHOOL FUND.

CHAPTER 30, SECTION 5.—The income arising from said fund so invested shall annually be appropriated for the support of public schools in the several towns.

Amount, 1905................................. $9,131 37

SHELL FISHERIES.

CHAPTER 853, SECTION 8.—The said commissioners may let and lease any land within the State covered by tide-water where the said water is of the depth of at least twelve feet according to the plats in the office of the commissioners of shell fisheries at the average low water, for the purpose of having the said land used in planting and cultivating oysters in the deep waters of Narragansett Bay and tributaries, at an annual rental of not less than five dollars per acre, for a term not exceeding ten years from such letting.

Amount, 1905................................. $47,087 26

CIVIL COMMISSIONS.

CHAPTER 29, SECTION 19.—Every person, other than those serving without compensation, accepting a civil commission under the State shall, at the time of receiving such commission, pay to the officer delivering the same two dollars for the use of the State.

Amount, 1905................................. $2,938 00

STATE INSTITUTIONS.

CHAPTER 291, SECTION 10.—They (the board of charities) shall, in their discretion, sell the products of said farm and institutions; they shall make such contracts respecting the labor of the inmates of the several institutions as they may think proper, and they shall cause full accounts thereof to be kept.

Amount, 1905............................. $54,352 41

HOME, DISABLED VOLUNTEERS.

CHAPTER 88, SECTION 15.—The General Treasurer is hereby directed to receipt to the board of managers of the National Home for disabled volunteer soldiers for such sum or sums of money as may from time to time be allowed as aid to the Rhode Island Soldiers' Home, which said sum or sums of money are hereby appropriated for the said soldiers' home fund.

Amount, 1905 .... $13,374 84

STATE HOME AND SCHOOL.

Sale of products, etc, under authority of annual appropriation act.

Amount, 1905................................ $600 45

COMMERCIAL FERTILIZERS.

CHAPTER 154, SECTION 3.—The manufacturer, importer, agent, or seller of any brand of commercial fertilizer, or material used for manurial purposes, the retail price of which is ten dollars or more per ton, shall pay, on or before the first day of April annually, to the General Treasurer, an analysis fee of six dollars for each of the fertilizing ingredients contained or claimed to exist in said fertilizer to be sold, offered, or exposed for sale within this State as aforesaid: *Provided, however*, that whenever the manufacturer or importer shall have paid the fee herein required for any person acting as agent or seller for such manufacturer or importer, such agent or seller shall not be required to pay the fee named in this section; and on receipt of said analysis fees, the General Treasurer shall issue certificates of compliance with chapter.

Amount, 1905............................. $2,436 00

TAX ON STREET RAILWAYS.

CHAPTER 580, SECTION 1.—For the purpose of providing additional revenue for the State, every street railway company incorporated under the laws of this State, accepting the provisions of this act, shall annually, hereafter, on or before October 1, pay to the State, a tax upon its earnings as follows, viz.: if the annual dividend paid by such company during the year ending on the thirtieth day of June next preceding the date of the return made according to law to the railroad commissioner for such year is eight per centum on its capital stock actually outstanding during such year, or less, or if no dividend is paid by it, the tax payable by it for that year shall be a sum equal to one per centum of its gross earnings for that year, and if such dividend exceed eight per centum then the tax payable by it for that year shall be a sum equal to the excess of such dividend over eight per centum; but in no event shall said tax be less than a sum equal to one per centum of such gross earnings, which shall be paid without regard to the net earnings of such company.

Amount, 1905............................... $60,478 12

INTEREST ON DEPOSITS OF THE REVENUE.

CHAPTER 33, SECTION 5.—He (the General Treasurer) shall deposit, subject to his order for the use of the State, all of the funds of the State received by him, in such safe and responsible bank or banks, trust company or trust companies, within the State, having a paid-in capital of not less than five hundred thousand dollars, as will give the greatest rate of interest therefor.

Amount, 1905............................... $3,157 76

PUBLIC LAWS.

CHAPTER 22, SECTION 8.—And (Secretary of State) he shall retain the residue in his office for sale at the actual cost price thereof, except as hereinafter provided.

Amount, 1905................................ $200 70

RHODE ISLAND REPORTS.

CHAPTER 16, SECTION 11.—He (Secretary of State) shall reserve such number of volumes for the use of the State as, in his opinion, is necessary, and shall, at his discretion, sell or cause to be sold the remaining volumes of the edition, accounting to the General Treasurer for the proceeds of such sales.

Amount, 1905............................... $1,315 00

MISCELLANEOUS.

Rents, sale of liquor and utensils forfeited, unclaimed money, agent State Board of Charities and Corrections, board and costs of certain insane patients, sale of office furniture, &c., Warden of State's Prison, fees and board.

Amount, 1905............................... $3,654 47

SALE OF TAX ASSIGNMENT ORDERS.

CHAPTER 303, SECTION 1.—The General Treasurer shall from time to time, whenever it is necessary, in order to provide funds for the current disbursements of the State, make and sell for cash to any person or corporation upon such terms as seem to him to be for the interest of the State, tax assignment orders, payable to order or bearer, and which are hereby made negotiable, of the whole or any part of the semi-annual installment of the State tax then next to become due and payable from any town or city, and the proceeds of such sale shall be deposited with the general funds of the State, and shall be available in payment of any appropriation lawfully made.

AUTOMOBILE, MOTOR CAR, AND MOTOR CYCLE LICENSES.

CHAPTER 1157, SECTION 1.—Application for registration of all automobiles, motor cars, and motor cycles shall be made to the Secretary of State, and with such application shall be deposited a registration fee of two dollars.

SECTION 8.—All money collected for registration and license fees and fines under the provisions of this act shall go to the support of public roads in this State, under the direction of the state board of public roads. And no fee shall be allowed or retained by said Secretary of State out of any money received by him under this act.

Amount...................................... $1,684 00

RESOLUTION AUTHORIZING GENERAL TREASURER TO BORROW.

WHEREAS, At a meeting of the electors in this State, held on the third day of November, A. D. 1896, the General Assembly was "authorized to provide for the borrowing, in addition to the amount of fifty thousand dollars, which it is now authorized to borrow, the sum of two hundred and fifty thousand dollars, or so much thereof, and in such installments, as may from time to time be necessary for the uses of the State;"

Resolved, That the General Treasurer is hereby authorized to make and execute in behalf of the State, from time to time, a note or notes, payable in gold coin of the United States of the present standard of weight and fineness, and not to exceed at any time, in the aggregate of such notes, the amount of two hundred and fifty thousand dollars, and to negotiate the same for a period of time not longer than one year, and at a rate of interest not to exceed four per centum per annum.

Passed June 2, 1898.

INDEX.

Lightning Source UK Ltd.
Milton Keynes UK
UKHW032254141118
332327UK00005B/176/P